Lyotard Reframed

Contemporary Thinkers Reframed Series

Adorno Reframed ISBN: 978 1 84885 947 0
Geoff Boucher

Agamben Reframed ISBN: 978 1 78076 261 6
Dan Smith

Badiou Reframed ISBN: 978 1 78076 260 9
Alex Ling

Bakhtin Reframed ISBN: 978 1 78076 512 9
Deborah J. Haynes

Baudrillard Reframed ISBN: 978 1 84511 678 1
Kim Toffoletti

Deleuze Reframed ISBN: 978 1 84511 547 0
Damian Sutton & David Martin-Jones

Derrida Reframed ISBN: 978 1 84511 546 3
K. Malcolm Richards

Guattari Reframed ISBN: 978 1 78076 233 3
Paul Elliott

Heidegger Reframed ISBN: 978 1 84511 679 8
Barbara Bolt

Kristeva Reframed ISBN: 978 1 84511 660 6
Estelle Barrett

Lacan Reframed ISBN: 978 1 84511 548 7
Steven Z. Levine

Lyotard Reframed ISBN: 978 1 84511 680 4
Graham Jones

Merleau-Ponty Reframed ISBN: 978 1 84885 799 5
Andrew Fisher

Rancière Reframed ISBN: 978 1 78076 168 8
Toni Ross

Lyotard

Reframed

Interpreting Key Thinkers for the Arts

Graham Jones

I.B. TAURIS

Published in 2014 by I.B.Tauris & Co. Ltd
6 Salem Road, London W2 4BU
175 Fifth Avenue, New York NY 10010
www.ibtauris.com

Distributed in the United States and Canada Exclusively by
Palgrave Macmillan 175 Fifth Avenue, New York NY 10010

ISBN: 978 1 84511 680 4

A full CIP record for this book is available from the British Library
A full CIP record for this book is available from the Library
of Congress

Library of Congress catalog card: available

Typeset in Egyptienne F by Dexter Haven Associates Ltd, London
Page design by Chris Bromley

Printed and bound by CPI Group (UK) Ltd, Croydon, CR0 4YY

Contents

To view a Glossary and extended Recommended Reading, visit
www.ibtauris.com/lyotardreframed

List of illustrations

Acknowledgements

I wish to thank Ashley Woodward, Jon Roffe, Simon Cooper and Karen Barker for reading draft sections of this work and their very helpful suggestions, and Robert Hastings for his help with the later stages of the text. Thanks go to everyone who lifted my spirits or helped me in some way during the writing of this book: Jane Landman, Mark Fraser, Sandra Corbett, Paul Atkinson, Stephen Zagala, Karl Trsek, Barbara Bolt, Ken Wach and Chili Naparstek. And, of course, the heroic Josh Nelson and Greg Staines who each bravely endured many film and pizza nights, and to Simon once again for all those morning coffees. Thanks also to my work colleagues, the campus librarians, and to my students, past and present.

I also wish to express my gratitude to the Melbourne School of Continental Philosophy who made a substantial monetary donation towards the licensing permissions for several reproduced images, and to the School of Applied Media and Social Sciences at Monash University (Gippsland) for their financial assistance.

Finally, thanks to my parents, Pauline and Ralph, and to Naomi Merritt for all her love and support (and drawing the theatre diagram and pulling the bibliography together).

This book is dedicated to the memory of Toadie the Pug for whom every mealtime was sublime.

Abbreviations

DF	*Discourse, Figure*
DIFF	*The Differend*
DW	*Driftworks*
HJ	*Heidegger and "the Jews"*
INH	*The Inhuman*
LE	*Libidinal Economy*
LES	*Lessons on the Analytic of the Sublime*
LR	*The Lyotard Reader*
LRAG	*The Lyotard Reader and Guide*
PC	*The Postmodern Condition*
PW	*Political Writings*
TRAN	*Duchamp's TRANS/formers*

These are works by Lyotard cited in the text. For publication details see the bibliography.

Introduction

What is called Philosophy of Art usually lacks one of two things: either the philosophy, or the art.

Friedrich Schlegel

The purpose of art is to lay bare the questions which have been hidden by the answers.

James Baldwin

When I see three oranges, I juggle; when I see two towers, I walk.

Philippe Petit

Let's talk a bit about art. Admittedly, it's never easy, but let's try. We'll begin with several examples of artworks, or at least things seemingly related to the arts.

The first is a painting of a black square literally called 'Black Square'. It is simply a canvas covered entirely in black paint – nothing more and nothing less. It was the first of several versions all bearing the same title and it is on display at the State Russian Museum in St Petersburg. It was painted by Kazimir Malevich in 1914 and constitutes a forerunner to the art movement called 'Suprematism'. The painting is valued at millions of dollars on the art market and is accruing more monetary 'value' every day (although the museum is unlikely to ever sell it). I know all of this because the information is written on a plate accompanying the picture in a book that I borrowed from the library. In fact, there are numerous other books written about the painter, his work, and the general artistic, historical and philosophical context for his *oeuvre* that I can consult should the need arise. Finally, I know that it is a truly 'great' work of art (can identify it is an artwork at all) because this library book tells me that it is and it was written by an 'expert' art historian who presumably should know about these things. Moreover, the painting is displayed in a special, culturally sanctioned place reserved for only the most worthy items – a place where it can be seen but no one may touch or smell (or lick?) it.

The next example concerns the work of Banksy, a mysterious graffiti artist who goes to considerable lengths to hide his true identity. Banksy has stencilled satirical images (usually 'appropriated' from popular culture) on walls and buildings in a number of cities over the last decade or so and during that time the images directly attributed to him have become sought-after collector's items with increasing monetary value. In fact, one recently sold for almost $200,000, although one might wonder to whom the money is being paid if Banksy's identity is unknown.

Attempts have been made by heritage groups and concerned cultural administrators to preserve some of these images by removing the part of the wall on which they are stencilled and thereafter moving them to more 'legitimate' spaces such as galleries or museums, or by leaving them where they are but identifying them with wall plaques as artworks worth preserving and covering them with a protective surface. In 2008 an image in Melbourne, Australia 'protected' behind such a transparent sheet of perspex was deliberately destroyed when someone poured silver paint between the protective sheet and the wall. Critics in the newspapers decried this as an outrageous act of vandalism (ironically, the same accusation that several city councils and shopkeepers had for years been directing at Banksy and other street artists for their supposed 'defacement' of public properties).

It is worth noting that Banksy's images often sit alongside images by other anonymous 'artists' (who don't even have the privilege of a 'fake' name or *nom de plume* in order to remain invisible or unknown). These images are regarded by those who highly value Banksy's work as without any monetary value at all. A couple of years ago, when confronted by a group of stencilled images on a wall, I asked a friend who was accompanying me if he could tell which image was Banksy's (although unbeknownst to him none of them were), and he admitted that he had no idea. The issue here was not what the image meant nor how technically proficient it appeared to be, but to whom to attribute its 'authorship' – because from the point of view of its monetary value the bankable brand name obviously matters. From my friend's perspective, though, all of the images that he saw were 'anonymous' (that is, unsigned) and therefore of equal (non-)value. So how then does one identify a 'Banksy' unless someone else – an 'art expert' – does it for you? But then, do you really need to know who the author of the work is in order to decide if you like it or not, or whether you find it interesting or engaging?

Now, around the corner from these same works in a little, secluded lane-way, was a wall covered in a 'different' kind of graffiti – seemingly meaningless swirls or blocks of colour attributed to gangs of roving, truant delinquents mindlessly defacing or defiling private property, public utilities, or 'communal spaces'. These 'tags' and doodles are usually regarded by almost everyone, apart from those who produce them, as worthless, anti-social, ugly, pointless, and as disrespectful of authority, the community, and of decorum in general: apparently, they are unambiguously irredeemable acts of 'vandalism', which involve damaging the property of others. To suggest that they have any artistic merit is usually treated with scepticism, if not outright disbelief.

One more example of a more personal nature: once, many years ago, whilst visiting a gallery in London, I found myself alone in a room confronted by an enormous abstract painting that had me intrigued yet left me perplexed. There was a wooden bench in front which I lay down on, hanging my head off the end, so that I could view the picture upside down in a manner that seemed somehow more suited to what I was seeing. Immediately a security guard (but let's be nice and call him a 'gallery attendant') entered and threatened to eject me for being 'disrespectful' towards the work on display, offensive towards other people (even though no one else was present), and abusive of the gallery as a public space. Of course, I denied the accusation and in reply he called me 'uppity', a 'dole-bludger', a 'vandal', a 'fascist', and also, somewhat contradictorily, 'an anarchist'. There was some irony to this as at the time as I was working several days a week as a part-time 'attendant' myself at another gallery located just half a mile down the road and, apart from preventing people from directly touching the works (a rule that the gallery insisted upon for insurance purposes and the broaching of which would have led to my instant dismissal), I never presumed to dictate any particular way that people should engage with the works. However, in this regard I was alone. The 'lesson' that I learned from the gallery owners, through the curators and other attendants, and even right down to their patrons, the 'clients' (or 'punters' as the curators and gallery owners rather quaintly referred to the public), was clear enough: that one should view the displayed art only in a reverential, quasi-religious manner. And indeed, this is usually how people do behave in galleries, tending to speak in soft, hushed voices (rarely laughing or joking – let alone crying), moving slowly from one work to the next, pausing for a half a minute or so, looking as if they are engaging in acts of respectful and contemplative worship. Indeed, it *is* very much like going to church...or a funeral.

Each of these examples raises important questions about art: what it is and how we recognise it, where and when it should occur or exist, what acceptable forms (whether legally or morally) it should take, who should have access to it and when, who is entitled to be called an artist or taken seriously as one, who evaluates the artwork's authorship or worth (and what type of worth that might be), how we should (or more often how we should *not*) engage with or respond to it (and where and when), what we might 'use' it for, and so on. These are not questions that can be addressed, let alone answered, in any simple way, and to avoid misleading you, I should state at the outset that this book does not directly address them, let alone provide 'answers' to the issues they raise. But rest assured that the underlying issues do remain ever-present throughout what you encounter in this book.

Finally, let's look at two further, less 'down to earth' examples, concerning two occurrences – two happenings – that took place in the same geographical 'space' but which were separated in time. Let's look at what sort of questions they raise.

First event: At 7.15 pm on Wednesday 7 August 1974, Philippe Petit, a 24-year-old acrobat and high-wire artiste illegally strung, with the aid of his friends and the use of a bow and arrow, a 450-pound steel cable across the 61-metre gap separating the 110-storey Twin Towers of the World Trade Centre in New York City, and then proceeded to tightrope walk between them. In contrast to the lengthy and secret preparations that preceded it, the walk itself lasted only a short time – barely 45 minutes – as he crossed back and forth at a height approximately 417 metres off the ground. When the police came to arrest him he ran between the towers, laughing and dancing on the wire. People down at street level looked up and watched in delighted or bewildered surprise. Eventually, facing the prospect of rain, Petit climbed down and was immediately arrested by the police.

Second event: Early in the morning of 11 September 2001 (9/11), a Boeing 767 jet, American Airlines Flight 11, commandeered by five al-Qaeda affiliated hijackers, crashed into the northern tower of the World Trade Centre. Approximately 17 minutes later another Boeing jet – United Airlines Flight 175 – was rammed into the other tower. Both structures collapsed shortly afterwards. The attack, which was almost a decade in the making, caused the deaths of almost 3,000 people including the passengers of the planes, 200 people who either fell or jumped to their deaths from the burning towers, and the hijackers themselves. Six thousand more were injured. When it happened, those who were not fleeing for their lives from falling debris looked on speechless in terrified or awe-struck disbelief, and for hours, days, even months afterwards people around the world struggled to make sense of what had happened as footage of the two crashing planes was repeatedly screened on television.

We could begin by asking what these two seemingly different events have in common besides the fact that they occurred in the same geographical 'space'. Well, to begin with, both were extreme acts in which the main participants risked or invited death directly or prosecution if captured. Each challenged an existing sense of what was possible or permissible: in the case of the first, a lone figure walking across a wire 110 stories above the ground; in the other, a small group wreaking devastation on the USA's own soil.

Each disrupted, to differing degrees and for different durations, the flow of daily existence, and derailed the structure and fabric of the social, political and ethical environment by constituting 'illegal' or transgressive acts. In the case of the first, Petit was immediately arrested afterwards; in the second, the perpetrators annihilated themselves in the act. One transgressed the laws of a community; the other, the ethics of a 'civilisation'. Each was in a sort of competition, a struggle in which they sought to triumph over an opponent (even if it meant destroying the rules of the game): the first was a game played by Petit against himself, a test of his own mettle, his own fear; the second the opening gambit in a 'holy war' directed against an economically and militarily more powerful foe.

Each 'set-up' involved enormous (although hidden) planning and preparation in its respective staging. Each was enacted primarily in order to be 'seen' (as a performance or spectacle requiring an audience). Both caused those who witnessed them to feel a range of intense emotions and to speculate about what had occurred and why. Each induced a sublime terror in the observers in respect to the risks involved and the price paid thereafter: the first, the fear attached to the privation of individual life; the second, the potential privation of a culture's future. Each intervened in and re-oriented an existing story: the first interrupted the smooth narrative of everyday life on the streets of New York; the second sought to hijack a global history, to challenge the grand, triumphant meta-narrative of Western civilisation.

In all these senses both occurrences constituted or marked 'events' – not in the sense that we might date-stamp them in a history book, but of somehow introducing an irruption or crack into the linear passage of time, an unravelling thread or kink that was 'witnessed' and yet which could not be easily understood, erased, smoothed over or forgotten.

Now the strange, comparative way that I have described these two occurrences so far might seem disturbing, but still you might wonder – what has any of this got to do with art? Well, let's ask Karl Stockhausen, the avant-garde composer. When he saw the footage of the destruction of the Twin Towers this is how he responded:

> Well, what happened there is, of course – now all of you must adjust your brains – the biggest work of art there has ever been. The fact that spirits achieve with one act something which we in music could never dream of, that people practice ten years madly, fanatically for a concert. And then die. And that is the greatest work of art that exists for the whole Cosmos. Just imagine what happened there. There are people who are so concentrated on this single performance, and then five thousand people are driven to Resurrection. In one moment. I couldn't do that. Compared to that, we are nothing, as composers, that is… (Stockhausen 2002)[1]

This statement shocked and outraged many people, even Stockhausen's most ardent admirers. Here was a well-respected and successful artist likening 9/11 – the destruction of thousands of lives and the wounding of many others – to a work of art, a concert, a spectacular orchestrated event, involving a conductor, a score, instruments, performers, an audience. As a result, and much to his own surprise, Stockhausen was almost universally reviled throughout the media as 'insensitive', naive, deluded, even immoral. He was accused of confusing art and reality, of being an apologist for mass murder or supporting the beliefs of terrorists, as out of touch (along with most contemporary art and artists) with the values and concerns of ordinary human beings, and of the needs of a society that ought to be shielded from suffering and the fragility of existence.

Now some people might be able to buy into the idea that Petit's walk constituted a kind of artwork – a performance piece or example of street theatre involving an actor, a stage, props, a script, an audience – even an artistic statement. But to liken 9/11, a terrible, horrific and wanton act of destruction, to an artistic statement or a work of art? For many people this was one step too far. As word spread about his comments and they were increasingly reported in the media, pundits and journalists wrote editorials and members of the public wrote letters to newspapers in response to Stockhausen's comments, many claiming that to even consider 9/11 in these terms was deeply offensive and potentially a sign of mental incapacity or emotional instability.

But why? Let's stop and think about this for a moment. Why can't the destruction of the Twin Towers of the World Trade Centre be considered an 'artistic statement' of sorts, given that it already shares a number of attributes in common with Petit's walk, or with lots of other cultural phenomena (such as Hollywood blockbusters with their spectacular special effects) – what makes it different? That the 'bad guys' seemed to win? That it involved mass murder? Because it was such a blatant and fervent 'political' blow? Or a moral outrage? Was it because it seemed such an anti-social, life-denying, even nihilistic act? Or that it intruded directly into our sense of the real and left a hole, a vacuum in its place?

But wait, does the inclusion of violence automatically prevent something from being a work of art? And what is violence anyway

– something done to the body, to the mind, to the soul, to speech, to our view of things? Is violence always unacceptable? What then of the police, the armed forces, or acts of self-defence? Is it simply a matter of context? Can a work of art then never involve violence – either depicted or employed? Must it always be apolitical, morally virtuous, life affirming, civilised? What of Picasso's *Guernica*? Or J. G. Ballard's novel *Crash* (or its filmic adaptation) which depicts people receiving sexual enjoyment from automobile crashes? What about Stelarc, the performance artist, who put hooks through his flesh and suspended himself in the air? Or Mike Parr hacking off his own (fake) arm? Or Carl Michael von Hausswolff's recent use of paint pigment mixed with the stolen ashes of Holocaust victims? Does even asking these questions about violence constitute an act of violence itself, an assault on our sensibilities? And what are the boundaries, the limits? Where and when are they drawn and where do they end? And why at one point and not another?

To some people, posing these questions might seem as equally offensive or ridiculous as Stockhausen's statement, but the moral outrage it invokes sidesteps, rather than addresses, the underlying issues. Whatever their moral import, Stockhausen's comments about 9/11 compel us to look more closely at many of our most cherished beliefs and assumptions.

However, I am not saying these things – walking this tightrope between the permissible and the intolerable, the legitimate and the illegitimate – in order to pass judgement on what took place or what was said about it. In fact, I am deliberately, if momentarily, suspending such judgement, because these questions (whatever their implications concerning 9/11) raise important issues about the way that society and individuals think about art. The aim of asking them – of briefly positioning art in relation to 9/11 – serves as a kind of limit-case, the seeming incomprehensibility of which reveals the fault lines in philosophy, politics, ethics and aesthetics, and makes us re-examine our own views as a result: about what art is and what it is supposed to do, about how it might challenge what we think we already know or believe to be true. Posing these issues enables us to ask, to consider and reflect upon the question not of what art says about 9/11 but rather, what 9/11 might say or suggest about art – to ask what it is about art (about what we think art is) that perhaps validates Petit's walk as a work of art and yet which precludes us from saying the same of the fall of the Twin Towers. That is, to ask, in the light of such a thought-experiment, why the lines that divide what is acceptable from the unacceptable, common sense from nonsense, the desirable from the repellent, or even pleasure from pain, are drawn in certain places rather than others – but also to ask how these boundaries might relate to what we expect (or don't expect) from art, or contribute to distinguishing art from all that it supposedly is 'not', and, perhaps most significantly of all, to wonder what kinds of 'legitimate' questions and provocations contemporary works of art can, should and do pose both to society as a whole and to each and every one of us.

The above questions and examples touch on many of the underlying issues concerning what art is and what it does that interest the French philosopher Jean-François Lyotard, the subject of this book. Repeatedly throughout his work Lyotard asks, not what do artworks *mean* (after the fact) but what *are* they and what do they *do* to us (what is going on when we actually encounter them)? Perhaps for many people the matter is already settled: they might claim that art civilises us, enriches us, makes us more self-aware, makes us better human beings, teaches us empathy, makes us more tolerant, provides us with moral guidance, that it entertains us or makes for a good financial investment. But these are not answers that satisfy Lyotard. Indeed, from his point of view they are not even answers at all. They already presume too much about what it is to be human, a subject, a person, a citizen, a thinker, a consumer, a society, a culture. Too many other questions already go begging. In the pages that follow we will travel alongside Lyotard as he poses his own questions and speculations about the nature and role of art.

But across several pages we have already travelled a long way, both in time and space, from blowing up skyscrapers in order to humiliate the West for its perceived injustices, to 'delinquents' spray-painting squiggles in an alley as a rebellious thrill, to people piercing their bodies or admiring car crashes or looking at paintings upside down, and in doing so we begin to see that these questions concerning what art 'is' and what it 'does' potentially touch and frame in conceptual, aesthetic, political and ethical terms, not just each of these extremes but all of the spaces between them – in fact, all shared social space. Moreover, it is a tense space in which seemingly incompatible and often incomprehensible elements collide or co-exist with few co-ordinates available for making sense of them.

This book serves two purposes: on the one hand, it provides an introduction for the uninitiated to the key concepts of the philosopher Jean-François Lyotard, whilst, on the other, it provides a commentary on and interpretation of his ideas about the arts for those who may already have some familiarity with his work. It is part of a series of books that examines thinkers on the arts and their respective views under the banner of 'reframing' or the 'reframed'. In respect to at least four of the figures in this series and their ideas – Lyotard, Heidegger, Derrida and Deleuze – this notion of reframing seems particularly apt, as each in his own way examines and questions what it means to frame something, to presume to provide a way of looking at and organising things in terms of an overarching mindset or conceptual paradigm or a 'meta-theory' (of giving it a definitive meaning or form or identity). In the case of Lyotard it will become clear that his entire approach is one that concerns the question of 'framing' and of 're-framing', of continually questioning such framing, not just in the form of a wooden border surrounding a painted canvas, or of a proscenium arch or cinema screen, a story arc or omniscient narrator, or a frame of film – but in terms of a meta-narrative, a 'theatrical' or phantasmatic staging, a device for channelling energy, a picture in your head, and so forth. He explores and questions how these are used to legitimate knowledge or understanding (i.e. what is acceptable and what is not; what is true and what is not; what we can and should agree on but also what we cannot), and how they control or regulate our sense of 'reality' – but also more importantly he asks how we might challenge and resist their power over us.

With the above concerns in mind, it is worth considering for a moment why Lyotard has been included in this series. This is an important question because many people (usually those with only superficial knowledge of his work) view Lyotard's ideas as *passé*, as concerning cultural debates and political issues no longer relevant. This situation has arisen I believe for two reasons. First, that his work became closely associated in the minds of so many with the word 'postmodern', a term that has fallen out of fashion in critical circles. This is somewhat unfair given that the notion of the postmodern advanced by Lyotard has little to do with the way most people use or understand this term and as such a case can be put, as we will see, not just for the concept's continued viability but for its indispensability.

The second reason, I think, is tied on the one hand to the economics that determine the production of knowledge – linked to issues of ideology, marketing, networking, publishing, university research profiles, grants, employment opportunities, etc. – which increasingly dominate and even re-organise the 'hamster wheel' that today passes for academia, and the vicissitudes of fame, celebrity and commerce – brand names, flashy exhibitions, corporate sponsorship deals, event management, the globalising of the art market – that have increasingly shaped the 'art' world, on the other. What unites them is an increasingly faddish obsession with chasing the 'next big thing'. As a result, Lyotard's work has, as with so many thinkers, been eclipsed by newer, more marketable theories or figures in intellectual and artistic circles – a situation not helped, of course, by Lyotard's lack of interest in self-promotion, or of making grandiose public declarations or playing along with society's insatiable desire for 'opinion'.

Fortunately, the last decade has seen a resurgence of interest in Lyotard's philosophy that has been slowly gathering momentum, largely due to the admirable efforts of James Williams, and more recent thinkers like Ashley Woodward and Keith Crome who, in building upon the earlier efforts of Geoffrey Bennington, Bill Readings and Andrew Benjamin, have put Lyotard's ideas back into circulation. This is to be welcomed, as Lyotard's work has been unjustly neglected on the whole. With this in mind, and given that the rubric of the 'reframed' series concerns the arts, particularly the visual arts, I have organised the text around, and devoted chapters to each of, the four key concepts in Lyotard's philosophical work that I believe most directly relate to these matters: namely, the figural, the libidinal, the sublime, and, of course, the postmodern. The book is organised in this way so as to emphasise the often neglected continuity that runs throughout these ideas and Lyotard's work overall. Thus the first and third chapters are devoted to exploring specific notions – the figural and the sublime, respectively – and the second and fourth situate each of these within the broader context of Lyotard's interest in the libidinal and the postmodern. These four elements provide the themes or threads that shape my discussion and the artworks that I discuss.

But before proceeding I want to provide, without pre-empting things too much, a brief taste of what is to come, by pointing to at least three inter-related concerns or themes that Lyotard repeatedly returns to in different ways throughout his philosophical writings. First, that art primarily concerns feelings (the way it makes us feel), and that it is always about feelings before it is about thinking or what has been thought. This is because we encounter art first through at least one of our physical senses (even words require our ears or our eyes to perceive them) and thus art directly affects the body before the mind. Secondly, that works of art are potentially transformative, able to disrupt our conventional and habitual ways of thinking and feeling. And thirdly, that an encounter with a work of art is often an event. As the first two claims seem relatively uncontroversial (although once we examine how Lyotard envisages these, that may no longer seem the case) something should perhaps be said about the last. The term 'event' recurs throughout Lyotard's *oeuvre*, in numerous contexts and inflected with many different traits or associations. One of the more common ways that it recurs concerns the possibility that art is an event, that it is something that we encounter or something that happens which eludes comprehension and representation, that in some way it is indeterminate or in excess of what we can grasp through perception or understanding, perhaps even something that dislocates or fractures our sense of time or selfhood. Yet nowhere in his work does Lyotard provide a *single* definitive account of what the word 'event' means. This, I think, is quite deliberate. He seems to suggest that defining it would somehow betray it, would leave out what is most important about it – so in refraining from giving it a precise, unambiguous meaning, Lyotard attempts instead to highlight certain things about the way language and human understanding work in general, and their inherent constraints.

In what follows I hope to show that Lyotard's work is still relevant, still provocative and challenging, still has more to offer than is usually acknowledged. Indeed, his work both revisits questions and issues that have not been (and perhaps can never be) exhausted and opens up new avenues of investigation as a result. It favours a diversity of approaches that extend beyond the narrow confines of traditional aesthetic concerns to compel us to think, to ask questions, and to be wary of settling for the first, easiest or most immediate answer that presents itself to us.

Chapter 1

The figural

> In art there is only one thing that counts: the bit that cannot be explained.
>
> George Braque

> The reality we can put into words is never reality itself.
>
> Werner Heisenberg

> To see with one eye, to feel with the other.
>
> Lyotard

In respect to the visual arts, *Discourse, Figure* is perhaps Lyotard's most dense and intriguing work. Written as his doctoral dissertation between 1966 and 1968, it introduces many of the core philosophical and aesthetic concerns that Lyotard subsequently pursued and reworked throughout his career. One of its most significant themes is the examination of the nature, role and viability of art, particularly in respect to the question of what 'theory' can offer in terms of supposed explanation or insight. Indeed, the very issue of what an explanatory model is and what it can hope to provide is fundamental to Lyotard's concerns, as is the related question of in what sense (if at all) language can communicate or capture those qualities indicative of the non-linguistic – that is, what are the inherent limitations of describing the pictorial in terms of the discursive? As such, *Discourse, Figure* is a critique of the limits of knowledge and representation and has significant implications for a number of contemporary fields, issues and debates – among which we could include the ongoing re-evaluation of the legacy of structuralism, semiotics and Lacanian psychoanalysis, as well as questions pertaining to the primacy (one might even say, the imperialism) of certain notions of 'textuality' and 'visual literacy' that pervade the humanities and are today still most prevalent in 'Cultural Studies'.

Discourse, Figure is prefaced with a series of, at first glance, seemingly disparate claims of which four are worth highlighting as a prelude to discussion. First, Lyotard claims that his book takes 'the side of the eye' and seeks to defend it (DF 5), but we might ask: defend it against what? The answer is from the 'I' and all that it entails – against the unquestioned dominance of thought, reason, certitude, consciousness, language, signification, recognition, order and stability (which marginalise or ignore feelings, the body, the unconscious, the sensuous, disorder, etc.). In short, it seeks to defend sensing and feeling from the totalising ambitions of discourse, knowledge, and understanding. According to his second claim, Lyotard situates his intervention within and against a history of the repression of the body and the senses and the privileging of Ideas (or concepts) and Reason that has characterised Western thought since Plato (DF 5). For the sensible, Lyotard insists, is neither a support for, nor simply an impurity within, the self-authorisation of thought and reason. Thus his third claim: that the sensible is not a 'text', it is not something primarily to be 'read', to be defined and understood, or subordinated to concepts, but something which by its very nature often eludes the certainties of such thought (DF 3–4). And finally, Lyotard describes his own approach to these matters as primarily a 'detour' intended to pave the way for a 'practical critique of ideology' (DF 14) – that is, as a means of exposing how these prejudices have installed themselves both within politics and everyday life (a claim that I will address at the end of this chapter).

Lyotard begins the general argument of *Discourse, Figure* through a phenomenological comparison of reading and seeing. He will revisit this contrast throughout the book in various different forms with the aim of first complicating this opposition and then deconstructing it.[1] Reading, he claims, is fundamentally 'discursive' and concerns language, textuality, signification and conceptualisation. It is 'flat' and involves fixed, commutative elements. Seeing, in contrast, is 'figural' and concerns plasticity, opaqueness, density and feelings. It is 'deep' and variable. The significance and implications of these terms will become more evident (and paradoxically less clear) as we proceed.

Reading is an act in which signification (and thus conceptualisation) is privileged. In our culture reading a text (whether it be a book, a painting, a photograph, a situation or even the very world before us) is a search for the recognisable meaning or clear idea that we believe resides within or potentially hidden behind what is encountered – a truth or message that awaits us. Reading is thus an act of interpretation, a decoding or deciphering of the text, defined as an extraction of concepts by way of signification, in accordance with the rules or conventions through which we believe it was formed or presented to us.

There is, Lyotard suggests, an inherent and colonising reductionism within this 'textual' perspective that characterises theory (and, by extension, discourse in general); it subordinates the material or sensuous aspects of such encounters to being merely supports for the recognisable concepts they convey. Yet over and over again, throughout his *oeuvre*, Lyotard will insist that art testifies to the inadequacy of this perspective, that there is more going on in a painting than the simple delivery or communication of a message – that we cannot explain a painting, or re-state a poem in prose, without fundamentally betraying those very expressive properties that first rendered it engagingly singular.[2]

Although the priority given to discourse, textuality and signification in Western culture becomes more obvious when words and pictorial elements are placed 'side by side' and the *signification* of the text potentially supersedes or overrides any potential ambiguity or opaqueness inherent in what we see – such as in a caption accompanying a photograph, or in the word balloons of comic books, or even in the case of the informational plaque or catalogue which accompanies an artwork – Lyotard actually has more than this in mind. For when we read a book, we are obviously first 'seeing' it, visually perceiving it as an object or collection of words prior to understanding what it might say or mean, but this act of seeing is somehow simultaneously elided: the reading of the written text subordinates and represses the plasticity or mutability of the visual.

What does it mean though to say that text represses the seen? Lyotard claims that we can only 'read' (i.e. decipher meaning) by no longer noticing or registering that what we are looking at are, in fact, graphic marks spatially positioned at invariable distances on a flat surface or on a support (such as a page). It is a crucial feature of reading that our attention does not dwell or linger on these marks (the letters) – which must be arranged in fixed and orderly spatial arrangements. Instead we see 'through' them to the signified meaning as if the words were transparent, functioning merely as windows opening onto another place (akin to Plato's realm of Ideas). In a sense, although letters and words are no less images than, say, a picture that might sit alongside them (although they are images that do not look like the objects they refer to), we disregard this aspect of their visual materiality in the act of reading them, of looking for the meaning which supposedly transcends their instantiation. Lyotard's point becomes more obvious when we consider that the letters of a word can take on a number of quite minor modifications or variations (changes in size, colour, font style, be printed or cursive, be misspelt or even leave some letters out) and, up to a certain point, it will make no difference to the legibility and more importantly, the intelligibility of the word's 'meaning'. The mind fills in what it expects to see based upon previous experience in an act of *recognition*. Thus, Lyotard's claim is that the 'plastic' or graphic element of writing is repressed in favour of the conceptual association of its discursive units – in a sense the 'letter' suppresses the 'line' from which it is constituted.

This repressed or occulted visibility is, Lyotard claims, the threatening 'other' of discourse. It is both a seeming impurity to be filtered out or elided, and simultaneously the very condition of possibility for reading: for one cannot read a text without in some way engaging with it through perception. It is potentially threatening because in those situations where it somehow asserts itself by becoming fore-grounded (i.e. the more we are 'distracted' from reading by the introduction of colour or contrast, the use of unusual typography, or unexpected spacing) the more disruptive of intelligibility and signification that it then becomes: in short, to linger on the line is to no longer grasp the letter, and this introduces an intransitivity that renders what is seen opaque.[3]

Lyotard calls this disruptive, 'troubling' aspect of the visible the 'figural' – for the visible is a figure that is both present within discourse and simultaneously external to it. In transgressing the identifiable units and the fixed intervals or spacings that constitute the text, it potentially de-stabilises the orderly arrangement of discourse, disrupts the communicative flow of information, and introduces a tension, a friction and density into signification and the act of reading. This tension arises, Lyotard claims, from the blocking together of these seemingly incompatible elements within the 'same space' – they somehow co-exist irreducibly in a paradoxical or incommensurable relation.

Before proceeding, it is worth pausing momentarily over these two terms, 'discourse' and 'figure', which Lyotard introduces. The term 'discourse' generally denotes the meaningful and formal arrangement of words for the purposes of communication and representation. But for Lyotard it also refers to the way that linguistic signs organise (according to the self-enclosed structure of language) knowledge and experience into a totalising system of concepts. In contrast, the 'figural', a term that both derives from and yet modifies the word 'figure' (and thus challenges its usual meaning of 'defining an outline', or providing a type of visual organisation), in Lyotard's usage, refers to transformations or interventions that visually disrupt discourse or violate the structure of textuality.[4] Perhaps though Lyotard should have rendered the word as 'dis-figural' because this more accurately suggests what he has in mind – that the figural is a sort of perceptual violence and cognitive vandalism or graffiti that disfigures, disrupts, distorts, defaces and deforms. It intervenes specifically at the level of *form* because this is the level of recognisability, the level at which we make cognitive judgements concerning what we already know or understand.

Lyotard further develops this initial contrast, between reading as the discursive use of language to convey concepts, on the one hand, and the figural as a troubling visibility, on the other, by suggesting that language and vision are each, in fact, premised upon, and characterised by, fundamentally different forms of negativity. The notion of language that Lyotard is referring to here derives from the work of the Swiss linguist Ferdinand de Saussure, whose theories provided the foundations for semiology or semiotics (the study of sign systems) and structuralism. To summarise quickly: Saussure argues that instead of examining language from an evolutionary viewpoint (as made up of numerous elements that are constantly changing) it should instead be viewed as a stable, virtual and self-contained system which exists as a totality from one moment to the next. This system (called *langue*) provides the underlying or unconscious combinatorial structure from which individual articulations or utterances (*parole*) are assembled and then actualised.

The structure of *langue* is composed of 'differences without positive terms' in which differential relations solely determine or differentiate the value of the inherent components: that is, the units or basic cells of language have no independent, intrinsic identity or pre-existing meaning of their own. Each of the units within this diacritical system derives its individual value from its relation to or difference from all the other co-existing terms – from the totality of virtual, simultaneously co-existing elements. At the most basic level these relational units are phonemic (i.e. the smallest sounds that we can clearly differentiate: b is not p is not c, etc.), sonic elements which can be combined to form words where a similar process of differentiation takes place (bat is not cat is not rat, etc.). It is at this level that differences of value make differences of meaning possible. These differences are correlated with an analogous process of conceptual differentiation. A helpful way to grasp this is to imagine perception and thought as initially two amorphous (undifferentiated) domains or continuous streams that co-exist without interacting. A grid or 'net' is thrown over them both and where it lands the strands of the net divide the two domains into a pattern of discrete bits, each bit now correlating a piece of one with a part of the other. In essence, distinction at one level produces a corresponding distinction or counterpart in the other level. The mind and the 'world' thereafter form a laminar relationship, but one determined by the 'net'. This net is, in fact, language, a self-enclosed system that produces signification rather than reflects pre-existing meanings. However, we should note that although the correlation of specific sounds and meanings is historically arbitrary in its origins, in terms of everyday usage once the two are linked the relationship between them is generally accepted thereafter as 'motivated' and thus 'fixed' (even if by unacknowledged convention).

Saussure also claims that the articulations of language are, in fact, signs. Spoken (and by extension, written) language is essentially a system made up of differentiated signs, and each sign is the respective point of correlation between the two domains mentioned above. Thus in Saussure's account a sign is a unity made up of two psychological parts which are in principle inseparable, like the two sides of a piece of paper. On the one hand there is a 'signifier', which is the psychological impression made by specific sensory input (such as combined phonemes or a written alphabet), and on the other there is the 'signified', the mental concept which correlates with this signifier. For example, the sign 'dog' (whether articulated as sounds through speech or inscribed as squiggles in the form of written words) conjures up a mental concept of a particular creature, ideally four-legged and furry that goes 'woof'. All meaningful experience is, according to Saussure, made up of elements – signs – that are both identifiably differentiated and yet combinable, analogously to the structuring of phonemes, according to certain social conventions. A key aspect of this account is that the object to which the sign is supposedly related (that which it 'stands in place of') is of little interest to Saussurean linguistics and, indeed, this is reinforced by the curious fact that within Saussure's account a sign such as 'dog' does not refer to a specific physical object but instead to the associated mental concept the signifier evokes.

Saussure's account was highly influential in subsequently shaping linguistics but also in its impact upon philosophy, the social sciences, literary studies, art history, etc., where it raised many important questions about the nature and role of social communication. Indeed, structuralism directly emerged from the attempt by a range of thinkers (such as Lévi-Strauss, Barthes, Lacan, Greimas and Todorov) to take these ideas about language – as a self-contained, differential and combinatorial, virtual structure that produces signs and delimits corresponding meanings – and apply them to all domains of human behaviour, cultural production and meaningful representation. Thus structuralism monolithically examined concepts such as fashion, cuisine, kinship systems, literature, cinema, even the 'unconscious' as meaningful, self-contained and universal, rule-governed symbolic systems analogous in their workings to spoken and written language: in short, as signifying texts able to be decoded and understood (i.e. 'read').

Now Lyotard partly accepts this influential model in which language is defined by relations 'without positive terms'; however, he notes that the systematicity of language here is premised upon a 'flat', self-enclosed, grid-like structure, in which the elements are distinguished and related by their oppositions (between specific units and between any given unit and the structure as a whole) and not, strictly speaking, by difference. Moreover, the structure of language functions in a manner akin to a table consisting of a series of horizontal rows and vertical columns in which its discontinuous units or cells are substituted in one direction and then combined in another according to specific codes or rules. Lyotard's point is that these units are related through fixed, unchanging (although virtually spaced) intervals and that this process is supposedly reflected in their instantiation in actual utterances. For example, the selection of a particular term in speech immediately excludes or suppresses by default any other possible terms from existing at that position in the utterance being assembled, and similarly with every subsequent position within it. In short, a sentence is a chain constructed from a series of such exclusions. Similarly, written text is organised in an analogous manner, inasmuch as the selection of any given word automatically excludes all other possibilities, and these selections are then arranged according to fixed intervals upon the page.

Lyotard describes this system of exclusions as the form of 'negation' that is characteristic of language as a sign system but he also argues that it makes no provision for explaining how referentiality takes place or can even occur: that is, that utterances somehow refer to 'things' or experiences (whether accurately or not) apart from language. Although we may not be able to comprehend anything without the mediation of language (even at the level of thought), this does not mean therefore that everything we experience is reducible to language. Moreover, because this is a combinatorial system consisting of finite, discontinuous and relatively interchangeable units, every possible combination and permutation is in a sense already accounted for (indeed, even predetermined) by the structure itself, and as a result nothing should be able to occur that is not contained within or prescribed by this inherent constraint on the range of possibilities. Language in the form described by Saussure cannot therefore account for contingent 'events', for unpredictable or unexpected associations, deviations of meanings, or effects (except as errors or confusions resulting from communicational 'noise'). It follows then that something 'else', not acknowledged within Saussurean or structuralist theorising, must produce these effects.

In contrast to the negativity of language that involves the opposition and substitution of discontinuous elements in a process of exclusion and elimination, Lyotard argues that visual perception is characterised by a different kind of negation. Vision, and here Lyotard draws upon the phenomenological studies of Maurice Merleau-Ponty, is premised upon a negativity related to mobility, synthesis and 'transcendence', but most importantly to *distance* as a constitutive spacing that is experienced as variability. It involves a constitutive and mutative spacing which links together terms without excluding other related terms.

In Merleau-Ponty's studies of perception he argues that the eye is neither immobile nor completely separate from the world that it 'sees'; indeed it is but one more moving element within a continuum (which he calls the tissue or 'flesh' of the world) that unites subject and object. In fact, perception, in Merleau-Ponty's view, is only possible because we are beings that have bodies, that we are embodied – not in a relation akin to piloting a corporeal ship (as Descartes famously described it) but as an inseparable and indistinguishable unity of consciousness and body. Thus the eye (as an extension of the body) does not merely see what is presented before it but is itself a mobile part of what is presented (continually changing its position) and thus affected by what is seen. The eye moves – both within its socket and in respect to the entire organism's ongoing motor activity – its 'reach' constituting a mobile field of interaction in which attentive point of view is directed yet ever-shifting. This visual field, made up of what the eye sees at any given moment in time, is a complex and ongoing construction. It consists of elements, linked to the observer's own presence as part of the scene, that move forwards or backwards, in or out of view, or which display or imply contiguous or overlapping 'facets' in respect to a 'horizon of transcendence'.

This notion of transcendence, which Merleau-Ponty borrows from the work of the phenomenologist Husserl, refers to the way that the things that we do not yet see, or cannot see in their entirety, are nonetheless implicated in what we actually do see: that there is an implied continuity in perception. This is evident in the way that 'objects' present certain sides or facets to us whilst hiding others.

For example, we cannot see the back of a cube without changing position, and indeed we cannot see all of its faces simultaneously no matter what position we adopt, yet we engage with it as an object that does have a 'back' and is a complete unity in itself. Through a combination of our movements and the retentions of memory we subconsciously synthesise (cognitively assemble and integrate) these changing views into recognisable objects situated within a seemingly 'objective' (or consensual) space that enables us to engage with them at variable distances. This sense of a homogeneous 'space' arises out of a heterogeneous and constitutive 'depth', which Merleau-Ponty suggests is primordial, and from which other spatial dimensions such as height, width and length derive. This depth – which situates our body, and fleshes out our world as a series of contiguous and overlapping relations that are not exclusive, and determines our 'distance' from the objects that emerge, move and hide within it – is 'invisible' in itself. It subsists as a transcendental difference from which the visible is born and yet which as potential is irreducible to being merely the antithesis of that which is visible. In short, it is the 'otherness' *of* the visible – the invisible that makes the visible possible.

Given that textuality involves one type of negativity being brought into contact with another, we can now begin to grasp in what sense the visible must function as a disruptive or tense figure within discourse, and how it can potentially destabilise or threaten the fixed distancing that underlies the intelligibility of text in terms of its material support. When both reading and seeing, letter and line, discourse and figure, are incommensurably and irreducibly blocked together in the same 'space', a radical otherness is potentially introduced.

Lyotard, goes further though, by suggesting that this negativity intrinsic to the visible, and the radical otherness which it constitutes, both invades and is presupposed by language in another important sense. There is a type of 'seeing' *within* language itself that can play a similarly ambiguous role, of being both disruptive of signification but also its necessary precondition, of being those very features of linguistic interaction that it seems to exclude yet which it must rely on for efficacy – namely, designation and referentiality.

Designation is a form of *indication*: it is when language functions as a kind of 'pointing', designating rather than signifying (i.e. standing in place of) aspects of the world. As Lyotard emphasises, language use, despite the arbitrary or unmotivated nature of the signifying elements that it draws upon, is not a completely abstract, indifferent, self-enclosed process. Language does not 'speak' itself but is used by, and embodied within, a speaker. It is deployed in specific situations and continually makes appeals to extra-linguistic phenomena. It is used to 'designate' features of one's environment, one's relation to that environment and one's feelings about that environment, and this process of pointing replicates the body's own possible distance to and from that environment in a manner that does not reflect the tabular structure of signification. For example, although in respect to the system of signs 'cat is not hat is not mat', when one attempts to draw another's attention to a particular cat (such as this specific feline sitting in front of me now) we rely on 'deixis' in order to achieve this. These are types of words such as now, you, here, there, above, later, etc., that denote positions in time and space but the meaning of which change or are transformed by the context in which they are used – and thus which do not operate in the manner described by Saussure's account. True, we can speak of a 'here' as opposed to a 'there' but the former's relation to a number of other possible locations is not reducible to such a straightforward positioning in respect to a linguistic structure (alongside, beneath, above, nearby, besides, etc.). Deictic terms do not function by a process of exclusion or elimination, but are instead dependent on contiguous relations derived from the visual field – a field (unlike the linguistic structure) which does not imply an indifferent, universal, almost disembodied positioning wherein the placement of the eye, and by extension the body, makes no difference to the oppositions that differentiate the linguistic units.

In this sense, 'pointing' is not simply the by-product of an enclosed signifying system, for it connects us to something extra-linguistic. Deictic signs join us to a sensory environment that is not reducible to simple oppositions, but which instead thickens and complicates our relationship to signification. In essence, through designation the 'visual' invades language, whilst also making signification itself possible inasmuch as it draws language outside of itself and grounds it in concrete instances of *parole*.

In a lengthy discussion of Stéphane Mallarmé's avant-garde poem 'Un coup de dés jamais n'abolira le hasard' ('A throw of the dice will never abolish chance', see Figure 1), Lyotard draws together some of these strands concerning mobility, spacing, distance, negativity and deictics, whilst revisiting once again his initial contrast between reading and seeing. He notes how the visible here introduces a figural element within the text, whilst also pitting referentiality against signification. Indeed, several different types of transformation of written language and signification occur that de-familiarise and deform them both.

First, what is particularly striking about this poem is the way that Mallarmé deliberately emphasises the plastic aspects of the printed text. Earlier I mentioned how the intelligibility of reading is premised on repressing the graphic qualities of the text, with some allowance being made for minor typographical infelicities or variations; Mallarmé, however, foregrounds these graphic aspects through the unconventional use of typographical features – such as different fonts, changes in the sizes of words, etc. – that deviate from our expectations and cannot easily be ignored (and which sometimes have little relationship to the meaning or importance of the specific words employed).

Secondly, and more importantly, he arranges the words in ways that seem to conflict with our usual manner of reading. Rather than positioning the words in a fixed and equidistant manner, he spaces them in radical and variable distributions (a 'mobile immobility') across the page. In this way he breaks up and 'disarranges' the text, violating the fixed spacing or coherent intervals of words that usually ensure the intelligibility of the reading experience. In doing so he compels the reader to linger over words and phrases – to become as aware of their expressive and seemingly contingent placement as of their meanings. Lyotard argues that this forces us to engage with the text in an unfamiliar and therefore estranging manner – the eye must slow down or jump about in unusual and exaggerated ways, giving itself up to the sensuous travails of space before the abstract generality of concepts.

C'ÉTAIT

issu stellaire

CE SERAIT

pire

non

davantage ni moins

indifféremment mais autant

Thirdly, through these transformations Mallarmé emphasises the referential dimension of language – that words serve to hold things at a fixed distance – but now this distancing itself comes to be the object of the encounter, disrupting the flat, tabular space of the signifying system itself and deconstructing the opposition between reading and seeing in favour of a more complex notion of difference. In doing so, Mallarmé foregrounds a key feature of modern art: that the embrace of art's supposed autonomy from social expectation ('art for art's sake') does not involve a simple retreat from or elimination of the world or objects but instead highlights the 'distancing' effect that the figure as visual referentiality usually introduces into discourse and which the latter then elides or subordinates (Carroll 1987: 35). In short, disarrangement becomes a means of focusing on the 'distancing' and transformative (i.e. figural) operation itself. We see not just the result but also the exposed workings of the process.

LE NOMBRE

EXISTÂT-IL
autrement qu'hallucination éparse d'agonie

COMMENÇÂT-IL ET CESSÂT-IL
sourdant que nié et clos quand apparu
enfin
par quelque profusion répandue en rareté
SE CHIFFRÂT-IL

évidence de la somme pour peu qu'une
ILLUMINÂT-IL

LE HASARD

Choit
la plume
rythmique suspens du sinistre
s'ensevelir
aux écumes originelles
naguères d'où sursauta son délire jusqu'à une cime
flétrie
par la neutralité identique du gouffre

1. 'Un coup de dés jamais n'abolira le hasard', Stéphane Mallarmé (1897).

The example of Mallarmé's style also draws attention to a different kind of 'seeing' that invades discourse. Lyotard, borrowing terms from Mallarmé himself, refers to this as 'poetic language' and claims that it serves a 'critical' function. This latter mode of using language, in which language is compelled to work against itself, relies on the use of rhetorical tropes and 'figures of speech' (such as metaphor, metonymy, synecdoche, irony, hyperbole, etc.) which displace or trump the literal or purely communicative and informational function of discourse. Instead they generate excessive 'lateral relations' that produce a greater range of expressiveness, of strange accretions and illogical associations that violently pervert or 'undo the code, without fully destroying the message' or its expressive 'truth' (the latter, for Lyotard, being not the text's conceptual content but instead its revealing of this transformational process at work).

These linguistic devices (later taken up and developed by Apollinaire and Marinetti amongst others) transform or twist meaning by either yoking together unlike concepts or by playing the designatory dimension of words off against their conventional significations, and by presenting unexpected associations, expressions and imagery. This is an effect that is crucial to Lyotard's claims, for this figural 'poetics' of the literary is one that de-literalises and disfigures discourse and 'deprives articulated language of its prosaic function of communication; [such that Mallarmé reveals]...in it a power that exceeds it, the power to be "seen" and not merely read-heard; the power to figure and not only to signify' (DF 61) – to 'see' seeing.

In summary, by stylistically disfiguring and destabilising established structures of meaning these devices and techniques introduce surprising and uncontainably transgressive 'events' into signification – they unhook the claw-like grip of discourse, causing language to spasm, quiver, throb and resonate.

Lyotard's discussion of Mallarmé also serves two other useful functions at this point. First, it provides an account of how works of art can be created within and from language itself

('Literature') – through an internal and creative transformation of the rules and expectations of discourse as communication – lest we fall into the trap of thinking that only pictorial forms count as potential artworks for Lyotard. And secondly, it provides us with the means of addressing the important issue, which I have deferred discussing until now, of the status of Lyotard's own theorising – for given his criticisms of discourse and interpretation, and given that he presents *Discourse, Figure* itself in discursive terms, where then does Lyotard situate his own discursive analysis of these matters?

This touches upon a key claim of Lyotard's: that just as we cannot abandon or completely sidestep language (and by extension thought itself) and still successfully communicate with others, so too can we never completely separate discourse and figure. They are unavoidably yet incommensurably and irreducibly co-present within all representation – and we cannot overcome this by simply ignoring one of the two or by reducing either one to the other. It is how we negotiate, exploit, and hopefully deconstruct this tense relationship that is crucial – how we show that ultimately the opposition between them is itself but a limited representation of a difference which differentiates, spaces and traverses them in a paradoxical relation. And here artworks, both visual and literary, provide discursive theory (and particularly theory which wants to 'talk' about artworks) with a means of undoing itself, of challenging its own colonising tendencies, and keeping open a mobile space within and between them.

The aim then is to take up these figural devices and to turn the language of theory against itself, pulling on loose or frayed threads that introduce spaces or holes through which strange events or effects might arise – to allow the creativity and artistry of art to transform theory in turn, in acknowledgement of the inescapable fact that a theory of art must at some point involve an art of theory, a kind of 'painting with words'. And *Discourse, Figure* should not be exempt from this lesson – it too should strive to transform and deconstruct itself. But as Lyotard himself acknowledges at the very beginning of the book, *Discourse, Figure* is in part a kind of 'failure' by necessity. For despite its deliberate intervention into, or 'working' over of, various debates about art, language and meaning, with each of its two main parts (devoted to phenomenology and psychoanalysis, respectively) exposing, harnessing and figuring tensions within theory itself, *Discourse, Figure* still remains a text that tries too much to signify, and, is still attached to systematicity and textuality – largely, one might add, because its style is still too discursively restrained.

Earlier I mentioned that Lyotard's stated aim was to deconstruct the opposition between discourse and the 'figure as visibility', to engage in a continual destabilisation of their relationship. This requires not only showing that vision (dis)figures discourse but also that discourse can in some way (dis)figure the visible, so it should come as little surprise that Lyotard subsequently turns towards examining visual perception in terms of its own structural features. Returning once again to Merleau-Ponty's phenomenological researches, Lyotard suggests that vision is itself subject to a certain amount of arrangement and organisation that functions in a manner analogous to the discursive, and that as a result vision can also, in turn, be figurally disrupted.

Interestingly, and in a curious reversal, several of the same features that functioned figurally in disconcerting language's orderliness and stability can also operate 'discursively' in respect to perception. For despite the differing kind of negativity upon which vision is premised, the workings of the eye and the visual field provide a structure analogous to the discursive that organises elements of the visible. More specifically it is 'attention' which prioritises what we focus on within the visual field.

For example, foveal vision is privileged in human experience, as focalisation occurs in the small area of the visual field aligned with its centre. This facilitates the attentive recognition of familiar objects corresponding to pre-existing concepts; for example, this is a chair like other chairs that I have seen. The general movements of the eye are thus subordinated to the identification of these objects through a process of synthesis in which objects are cognitively – though unconsciously – assembled from the 'aspects' they present (for example, seeing an object from different sides allows us to 'increasingly' isolate it within the visual field, to extract it from an otherwise continuous background and thus render it accessible). Similarly, gradations of tone, modulations of colour and the juxtaposition of planes, differentiate and structure the realm of what is seen, and contribute to organising the space in which objects are experienced, thus reinforcing the impression that the visual field is stable, coherent, homogeneous and unified.

Historically, Western culture has sought to 'replicate' this attentive type of vision through the development of various pictorial conventions. These conventions both derive from, and also mutually sustain, a dominant conception of how vision takes place that Merleau-Ponty finds particularly objectionable.

The basic problem is that the conventional view of seeing is premised upon a peculiar fusion of philosophical and scientific models of optics that are correct in their mathematical principles and physical details concerning the movement of light, yet misrepresentative of how seeing is actually experienced. This model of vision is one that goes back hundreds of years and has exerted, and still exerts, enormous influence. It is based upon the assumption that the eye is the passive and immobile recipient of light. As such it describes vision in abstract terms as simply the convergence and imprinting of straight-moving light rays upon the retina of the eye.

Its artistic correlate can be found in the principles of 'point' or linear perspective that have dominated Western art for the last 600 years. These principles, which arose during the Quattrocento based upon the experiments, works, methods and teachings of Masaccio, Alberti, Dürer and da Vinci, exploit and exaggerate certain visual features and optical effects such as changes in size and the exaggerated use of foreshortening, so as to enable the 'translation' of the outlines of three-dimensional objects onto a two-dimensional surface.

The most important of these pictorial techniques involves the direct or implied representation of geometrically straight lines, arising from one or more 'vanishing' points converging upon an implied horizon within the picture plane, so as to suggest the arrangement of objects in space and to generate a related sense of volume or depth. This picture plane is an imaginary rectangle that reflects an identifiable image by presenting the contour of a depicted object and the parts it circumscribes as corresponding point for point on a greater or smaller scale (and depending on the size of the representational surface) to the original three-dimensional object – for example, Dürer's famous 'metal grid' was a device specifically designed to both reflect and facilitate this process of 'translation'.

These fundamental principles and techniques were supplemented over time by the use of other techniques such as colour contrast and tonal modulation. The basic aim of these collective techniques was to improve the accuracy of the supposed mimetic qualities of pictorial representation (i.e. to show things as they really 'are' or present themselves to us), and thus they provided a system of rules that, once learnt and assimilated, enabled observers to code and decode (i.e. to read) pictorial images in consensual ways.

Against this view, Merleau-Ponty argues that the visual field and the lived perspective through which we grasp it, is 'not a geometrical or photographic one'. Moreover, the traditional techniques of perspective by which we represent visible objects are merely conventions and not accurate renderings of how we see. Putting aside the fact that the traditional view of vision and the development of linear perspective derive from a model that discounts the importance of movement as the basis for perceptual and cognitive synthesis (and the obvious fact that, physiologically, vision is binocular – thus already presenting two different perspectives prior to their cognitive synthesis), it is obvious that this is an 'idealisation' abstracted from mathematical concepts. We can grasp the essence of Merleau-Ponty's criticism if we note the simple fact that the one, two and three-point types of perspective used in Western painting are not universal means of organising the picture plane. They are, in fact, conventions historically and culturally specific to Western cultural development and the primacy of a specific notion of 'realism'.

For example, briefly consider traditional Chinese art. Here the distance of a depicted object from the 'observer' of the representation is indicated through the positioning of the object either towards the top of the manuscript (i.e. as supposedly 'further away' from the viewer) or at the bottom (and thus as 'closer' to the viewer) with little consideration for changes in the size of the object – something which Westerners find odd and often dismiss as 'unrealistic'.

This 'axiological' type of perspective was not simply a matter of arbitrary historical and aesthetic contingency but clearly served a social or ideological (i.e. 'motivated') purpose within and specific to Chinese society, just as 'flattened' figurative forms did in ancient Egypt, and linear perspective still does today in Western representation. What is striking is that each of these examples involves a recognisable structure or support around which social, political and aesthetic ideas can be organised: in short, a 'good form' and a set of conventional illustrative rules that ensures communicability and potential social and political consensus concerning 'experience' – what is perceived and understood.

Merleau-Ponty's own account of perception, which Lyotard largely embraces and sets against the primacy of the model of linear perspective, sees the visual field as, in fact, curvilinear and thus at odds with the prevailing conventions of perspective. The visual field is curved, warped even, and what appears at its margins presents an 'otherness', a play of the visible and the hidden that continually undoes or threatens the primacy of the foveal centre of attention and the general structure of vision. However, rather than constituting a blurred region that simply awaits being brought into focus, this margin, potentially at least, remains indeterminate in its status as a constitutive part of vision. It presents potential positions from where things do not look unclear but rather appear different. Within this edge or fringe the world is continually rewoven – it is not a collection of pre-existing objects that simply moves in and out of view but which are born, shaped and dissolved. It provides 'access' to a 'depth' from which empirical vision is subsequently derived.

Lyotard refers to this figural otherness within vision that 'troubles' its discursive-like structure and its systematicity as anamorphic and cites Holbein the Younger's famous painting *The Ambassadors* as an example (see Figure 2).

Holbein's painting depicts the two wealthy men who commissioned it standing beside a table on which sit numerous objects (a bible, an astrolabe, a lute, a compass, globes, scrolls, etc.) intended to exemplify their cultural and economic capital. The picture is unusual in that spread or stretched across the bottom of the image there is a seemingly amorphous smear or blot. Or at least this is how it appears from the front, from the usual geometric point that defines linear perspective. However, if the viewer adopts a lateral viewing position – to the side of the painting – and looks awry at this anamorphic element (i.e. with a sideways glance in which the rest of the painting can no longer be grasped as a totality) then the smear 'decompresses' into the image of a skull.

Numerous commentators over the years have advanced different explanations and interpretations of the picture in general and of the skull in particular, based on the painting's history and constituent parts, as well as the biographies of Holbein and the two courtiers it depicts. However, for Lyotard, what is important about *The Ambassadors* is the way that its anamorphic qualities reveal the trace of the figural as a disruptive force. Anamorphosis introduces a resistance or friction into the supposed constitution of the painting as a perspectival arrangement of 'unified' space (where the latter is analogous to the discursive); it presents a figural element that subverts the subject-matter's meaning and affirmation of civilisation, power and immortalisation and which undermines the painting as a space that can easily be read because the 'signifier is itself under siege, overturned under our own eyes' (DF 380).

Another interesting example of the tension between discourse and the figural, that also playfully highlights many of the issues discussed so far, can be seen in two related works by René Magritte, *La Trahison des Images* ('The Treachery of Images') and *Les Deux Mystères* ('The Two Mysteries'), painted roughly 38 years apart. The first painting depicts the image of a smoker's pipe accompanied by

2. *The Ambassadors*, Hans Holbein the Younger.

text painted underneath it in the semblance of handwriting which reads *'Ceci n'est pas une pipe'* ('This is not a pipe').

In this painting we see the image of a 'recognisable' object accompanied by a caption that seemingly affixes a meaning to what is seen: that 'this is not a pipe'. But the caption seems at the most obvious level to contradict what the picture actually shows. We *do* 'see' a pipe (subject to certain pictorial conventions), so the statement seems false. If we take the words to be pointing to or designating the pipe, they are also false. However, if we take the words to be referring to themselves then it is true that they are not a pipe and nor do they resemble one. If, though, we take the words to be referring instead to either the image of the pipe or the painting itself, then the claim is also true because they are not, strictly speaking, the object. The words here are *not* the thing (the referent or original object depicted), but neither is the visual image – hence their treachery, for they are both merely images or signs.

Yet in both cases the signs stand in place of an object whilst evoking a mental concept of that object: neither the words nor the image is a pipe but the words and the image *of* the pipe are somehow both structured discursively – they signify a concept to be decoded and this constitutes a text to be 'read'.

In the first painting there is a complex movement, back and forth, taking place between reading and seeing. The second painting, *The Two Mysteries,* introduces further challenges (see Figure 3). To begin with it incorporates the first painting within itself, in what initially appears to be a straightforward act of self-reflexivity. It depicts the earlier painting resting on an easel in a bare room (possibly an art gallery or studio). More significantly, what sets this painting apart from *The Treachery of Images* is the presence of the image of yet another 'pipe' above and to one side of the easel. In the original painting the image is quite 'flat' – there is a minimum of tonal modelling used in depicting the pipe's shape – however, there is nothing in the image to contradict the impression that it is simply resting on a surface of some kind. In the later painting, in contrast, the additional pipe seems present but in some indeterminate way, for it is unclear whether it is floating in space without any visible means of support or merely painted on the wall behind. Despite the depiction of floorboards in the foreground receding towards an implied horizon (thus introducing spatial arrangement according to linear point perspective), this spectral pipe defies our expectations of its placement in the image. Like the skull in Holbein the Younger's *The Ambassadors*, it anamorphically disfigures the organisation of the picture as something to be read and thus understood.

So far we have examined Lyotard's claim that visual works disrupt or introduce a certain otherness into signification and how in turn vision can itself be disrupted, but now we must finally ask

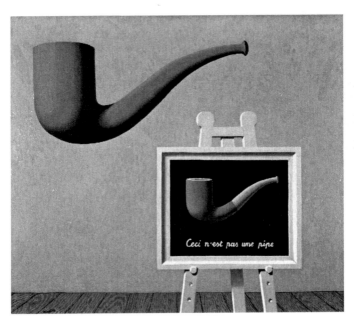

3. *The Two Mysteries*, René Magritte (1966), oil on panel.

from where does this otherness arise? What is its 'source'? For Lyotard it is 'force' that disrupts or violates both discourse and perception, and the basis of this force is desire. Turning from the phenomenological concerns of the first half of *Discourse, Figure* to psychoanalytic theory in the second, Lyotard finds in Freud's account of the unconscious, primary processes and the notion of libido, a theory of energetics directly linked to the body that is able to account for the workings of the figural.

Crucially, Lyotard identifies in Freud's work two competing and, at first glance, seemingly incompatible theories of desire: desire as force (or libido) and desire as wish. Basically, the first is an energy characterising psychic functioning that is both in excess of, and not intrinsically attached to, any given object, whereas the second is an attempt to phantasmatically grasp or immobilise the object that it lacks. This initial distinction will become more complex as we proceed. Indeed, we will see that desire is marked by a radical ambivalence in which these two types of desire are conjoined: that desire already contains within itself its own prohibition. In order to grasp why this distinction between two types of desire is so important for Lyotard and what bearing it has on the figural, we need to take a brief detour through psychoanalytic theory.

Freud's development of his theory of desire and the psyche was premised on the deduction of the 'existence' (or insistence) of an unconscious solely from its residual empirical traces – that is, seemingly disruptive effects upon conscious thought and behaviour in the form of slips of the tongue, peculiar physical symptoms, memory lapses, dreams, etc. In particular, Freud's investigation of dreams led to the formulation of his first account of psychic functioning, the so-called 'topographical model'. In this model Freud distinguishes between, on the one hand, 'consciousness' (moment-to-moment awareness which is closely tied to the perceptual system) together with the 'preconscious' (wherein certain memories and ideas are stored but can be recalled depending on their nature and the circumstances) and, on the other hand, the workings of the 'unconscious' where certain perceptions, associations, memories, ideas and feelings are inaccessible (i.e. held back or repressed from consciousness and the preconscious).

Freud further describes this psychic duality in terms of a distinction between different regimes of psychic activity that he labels the primary and secondary processes. He characterises the unconscious in terms of these primary processes that consist of the continual shifts of a freely mobile energy within the psyche that he calls 'libido', and which can potentially be invested in, bound or attached to various perceptions, ideas, memories, objects and actions. In Freud's formulation this libidinal energy is subject to the demands of the so-called 'pleasure principle', wherein uncomfortable increases in energy related to unconscious and usually socially unacceptable urges are discharged (in the absence of a real object) through some kind of acceptable hallucinatory or phantasmatic substitute or compromise-formation. Later Freud came to describe the infant in respect to this energy as 'polymorphously perverse', because in principle this energy could be attached to any type of representation within its psyche, although he saw the individual organism more typically as passing through a series of stages in which its libido was bound to a succession of specific types of 'objects' – such as the oral or anal. In summary, Freud characterises the activity of the primary processes as non-rational, and as fundamentally organised around the desire for immediate gratification and the ready abandonment of reality for phantasmatic substitutes where such gratification is otherwise unavailable (although he also later came to suggest that the unconscious is devoid of any inherent sense of time's passage or sense of negation or finality).

In contrast, secondary processes, which encompass the binding and structuring of the libido, enable linear thinking, planning and reasoning: for as libidinal energy becomes increasingly bound or invested over time in relation to ideas, perceptions, memories etc., the secondary processes that characterise consciousness and the pre-conscious develop out of the disorderly primary processes. In this sense the secondary processes constitute an emergent structure that both covers over and attempts to regulate the activity (the energetic discharges) of these internal processes. But it also evolves as an adaptive armour or set of defences consisting of associations, habits and responses which, expressed primarily in the form of verbalisation and motor activity, help the organism thereafter to cope with its external environment. It is the regulative and orderly aspects of these secondary processes that provide the organism with a capacity for logical planning, for socialisation, and the ability to defer gratification of basic urges and desires subject to the 'reality principle' (i.e. the need to adapt to conditions external to the organism). In short, secondary processes are built upon (and thus obscure) primary processes, but more significantly, they found and organise conscious thought. However, it is important to note that the primary processes are not neutralised by the emergence of the secondary processes – merely provisionally contained for the sake of survival. Strictly speaking, unconscious libido is in excess of, and at odds with, secondary processes; it is antithetical to discursive structure despite being subject, to some degree, to the latter's constraints.

Lyotard claims that libidinal energy accounts for how representation and the figural relate to one another, and suggests that we can discern the fundamental workings of libido in the seemingly anarchic nature of dreams. Indeed, much of Lyotard's subsequent argument in *Discourse, Figure* derives from his examination of the implications of Freud's own analysis of dreams as the 'royal road to the unconscious'. In *The Interpretation of Dreams* Freud posits that repressed thoughts and feelings exert hidden or disguised influence or pressure on our mental repesentations, and this 'interference' leaves more noticeable traces whilst we are asleep when the barrier holding back such repressed ideas and feelings is weakened. This led Freud to propose that dreams are types of wish-fulfilments, visualised phantasies triggered by contingent and resonant associations between recent waking experiences and past unresolved issues or emotionally charged memories. They allow dangerous or traumatic thoughts or socially unacceptable urges to achieve a displaced or compromised fulfilment through a variety of distorting or transforming mechanisms – that is, the latent trigger is transformed into a less threatening 'wish' or desire that can in this different form achieve a kind of relatively satisfying expression that does not disrupt sleep.

From Lyotard's point of view one of the most important notions in *The Interpretation of Dreams* is the crucial distinction that Freud makes between the 'dream-work' (what the dream does: its underlying workings) and the actual 'dream-thoughts' (what the dream is about) that the former transforms. He sees this as a far more important distinction than that existing between *latent* content (the original motivating thoughts of the dream) and *manifest* content (what we remember of the dream upon waking). The dream-work is the 'working over', the transformation of the material presented in the dream and this, Freud claims, is the dream's essence: that it functions as a 'workshop' in which dream-thoughts are transformed by various mechanisms that we will examine shortly.

Because Lyotard is proposing that the workings of the unconscious are solely energetic and argues that discourse is related solely to secondary processes, this brings him into direct conflict with Jacques Lacan's account of the unconscious (keeping in mind that the latter was more influential at the time when *Discourse, Figure* was written than perhaps it is today). Lyotard is utterly opposed to Lacan's re-writing of the unconscious in terms of notions derived from structural linguistics, particularly Lacan's infamous claim that 'the unconscious is structured like a language' which characterises the psyche in terms of discursive features and functions.

A brief synopsis of Lacan's view will help clarify the differences between their respective positions. Taking note of Freud's repeated emphasis on the relationship between language and the expressions of the 'unconscious' in the form of parapraxes, jokes, rebuses, speech dysfunctions, the 'talking cure', etc., Lacan claims to be updating psychoanalytic theory in the light of Saussurean and structuralist insights into language, discourse, and signs, of which Freud was unaware.

He argues that the overall structure of the psyche is analogous to language itself (i.e. a structure of differential relations), and even made up of certain privileged elements derived directly from the language system – namely, signifiers – subject to similar rules concerning their selection and combination. Unlike Saussure, however, Lacan claims that the bond between signifiers and signified is not fixed or unified but rather one of disjuncture, in which considerable movement or sliding of one 'over' the other takes place.

The principle innovation Lacan introduces is his claim that mental functioning is made up of chains of signifiers (sets of elements from the level of the phoneme upwards). Repression, rather than being an energetic process, involves the relevant signifier being excluded from consciousness. This signifier no longer presents itself as a direct link in the signifying chain (the sequence of associations informing the conscious thought) but instead falls from view and functions thereafter as a traumatic element that is still somehow 'influentially' attached to the chain without appearing as a linear link within it. Such 'repressed' signifiers over time form virtual links among themselves and it is this process that Lacan defines as forming a structural 'unconscious' (existing not 'inside' a given individual but trans-subjectively in relation to how each individual relates to or intersects with, language as a pre-existing social symbolic system).

Lacan uses Freud's famous anecdote concerning the 'fort-da' game as an exemplary support for his argument (an example that we will revisit in the next chapter). In this account Freud interprets his grandson's repeated attempts at throwing a cotton reel tied to a piece of string from his cot (crying 'Fort':

gone) and then retrieving it (crying 'Da': there) as an attempt to assuage anxiety caused by his mother's absence. Lacan, in contrast, emphasises the way in which the dialectic of presence and absence which characterises the trauma is inscribed within language via opposed signifiers (in this case, the phonemes of 'o-o' and 'a-a') and thereafter structures desire, thus paving the way for the structural unconscious.

In this manner, he uses structural linguistics and semiotics to strip Freud's theory of its energetic substrate (libido and primary processes). In his new account of the psyche, Lacan views both conscious and unconscious aspects of the human organism (which he now refers to as the 'split subject') as merely derivatives of the structural organisation of elements of language: the unconscious is a particular arrangement of signifiers. By extension, dreams are also the products of such linguistic mechanisms and Lacan is obliged to explain how this can be the case. His account of dreams, and signifying processes more generally, draws upon the claims of the structuralist Roman Jakobson, that thought (as a reflection of internalised language) is characterised by two axes or operations: the selection of meaningful elements (vocabulary) and their combination (syntactical), which the latter exemplify through the workings of rhetorical devices such as metaphor and metonymy.

In his theory of dreams, Freud speaks of four mechanisms through which latent (potentially distressing) thoughts or urges are converted into the more acceptable (i.e. less threatening) manifest content which we remember on waking: these are 'displacement', 'condensation', 'conditions of representability' (or figurability or symbolisation, in some translations) and 'secondary revision'. Lacan is only interested in the first two as these reflect his primary concerns. First, Lacan aligns metaphor and metonymy with the Freudian mechanisms of condensation and displacement. Condensation he links to metaphor, which he defines as one term substituted for another (wherein the original term remains, although hidden, still virtually present and efficacious), and displacement he links to metonymy (or more accurately, synecdoche), where a part of something is used to stand in place of the whole (for example, 'give me a hand' where hand stands for an entire person). Lacan's aim is to generalise these two 'linguistic' mechanisms not just as explanations of the dream-work but also as a means of explaining the production of subjectivity, of desire and all the most fundamental workings of the unconscious. Indeed, these are the bases for Lacan's respective theories of the split subject and of how desire is generated and its fulfilment endlessly deferred.

Lyotard completely disagrees with Lacan's account. He makes very clear his own view that the unconscious has nothing to do with the discursive or the 'defiles of the signifier', rejecting the claim that the operations of the dream-work or the unconscious are linguistic mechanisms or even indicative of a language-like structure. Instead, he argues that they are fundamentally at odds with such organisation, thus reiterating Freud's important claim, which Lacan ignores, that what is important about a dream is not the content of the dream itself but its 'work'. It is the dream-work as a 'working over', a transformation of material, that is significant, and this material arises from a combination of the day's residues and memories or past ideas that the former evoke and resonate with. As such, the content of the dream does not arise from the 'unconscious' but out of a mixture of conscious *and* preconscious elements to which something is then done. In other words, in Lyotard's view, the dream is not a translation from one region to another, or one language to another, or even from one set of signifiers to another, where in each case one of the two is otherwise hidden from or inaccessible to consciousness, but instead the dream-work, the unconscious workings of the primary processes, is merely a set of operations enacted upon the content of the conscious/preconscious system whilst we are asleep. As the title of the relevant chapter in *Discourse, Figure* (which is itself a quote from Freud) baldly states: 'the dream-work does not think'; instead it is what is done to thought. There is no unconscious apart from the operations of these mechanisms on conscious and preconscious perceptions, ideas and memories, and the transformations they produce – for these operations are but energetic expressions of the primary processes. It is true that the workshop of unconscious desire, creates a phantasmatic, representational space from the fragments of conscious and preconscious experience but it does not reside within this same space – as we will come to see shortly, it exists in no place.

Lyotard emphasises the malleability of these transformative processes, particularly displacement and condensation, because they are indicative of libido, and thus the working of the primary processes in general. In his account, which is more faithful to Freud's own than Lacan's, Lyotard characterises displacement as the movement of energy from one representation (or part of a representation) to another and condensation as the compression of something into a smaller volume or space. As an example of the two working in tandem, Lyotard describes a piece of paper containing text which is then crumpled up so that the words, or particular letters, which were originally distant from one another now appear closer together in new seemingly 'meaningful' combinations.

In respect to Freud's other two mechanisms, Lyotard suggests that 'the conditions of representability' concern the indifference of the energetic drives to the type of content being transformed (thus both images and words can be appropriated and treated as equivalent and interchangeable raw material), and 'secondary revision' concerns simply the residual effects of the importation of material from secondary processes (the conscious/preconscious system). In respect to the latter, on awaking the fragments of the dream are 'narrativised' (placed in a sequence that suggests causal relations without providing them) through their subordination according to the dictates of discursive or conceptual thought.

It is important to fully grasp why Lyotard places such emphasis upon Freud's account of dreams. The key point is that the two primary mechanisms of the dream-work, condensation and displacement (which also characterise the primary processes more generally), are the same mechanisms that characterise the 'interference' or workings of the figural. Indeed, Lyotard suggests that there is a 'radical connivance between the figural and desire' indicated by the effects of the primary processes upon the secondary processes: 'The essential characteristic of the figures to which desire gives rise, in language as well as in the field of vision, is that they disconcert recognition...they allow themselves to be recognized as unrecognizable' (DF 282). The value of the dream-work then is that it provides us with a crucial insight into the operations of the figural 'workshop' that applies not just to dreams, or even to art, but to all forms of representation, and Lyotard views these transformations as functioning at three levels (which roughly correspond to the workings of consciousness, the preconscious, and the unconscious, respectively).

The first level is that of the 'figure-image'. This pertains to the 'visible' object and the diffusion or violation of its outline or contour: 'what suffers abuse here are the rules regulating the formation of the perceived object...what it deconstructs is the silhouette's outline; it is the *transgression of the contour*' (DF 274). In other words, it concerns the dismantling or defacing of the recognisability of the object as image. This can take place through the multiplication, dissolution, subtraction or erasure of the defining outline so that the space that it occupies, or its relation to its immediate surrounding objects or environment, is blurred or confused. The example that Lyotard uses to illustrate this is Picasso's sketch *Etude de nu* (Study of a Nude), although perhaps a better known example might be Marcel Duchamp's *Nu descendant un escalier n° 2* (Nude Descending a Staircase, No. 2), where we see the outline of the figure dissolved through its multiplication.

The second level is that of the 'figure-form'. This concerns the transgression of the general form or nervure of the scenography or structure or support of what is visible – whether this be in respect to the *mise en scène* of a film, the use of perspective in a painting, or the stage-machinery of a theatrical play. Form is essentially the level at which our seduction by phantasy is usually enabled and indeed the sort of organisation or schema that is in question here is one that we are usually unaware of (as it is seemingly hidden or obscured), although it can be brought to our attention with some effort, or through its transgression. The example of a transgression of figure-form that Lyotard provides is the 'action' painting of Jackson Pollock where the eye no longer has any co-ordinates for organising what is seen into a meaningful scenario or unified space. He even suggests that Pollock's work evokes, through its use of drips and splashes of colour, traces of the pulsional forces of the energetic primary processes.

The third level, the 'figure-matrix', concerns the enigmatic 'source', the cauldron from which both phantasmatic images and forms derive (and from which they are also dismantled). This is the most difficult to describe because it is has no clearly defined conceptual correlate and thus no direct examples of it can be given – it is unrepresentable within either speech or perception. However, Lyotard's choice of the term 'matrix' – deriving from the word '*matrice*' and thus suggesting the 'maternal' womb – gives us some clue as to its nature. This relates back once again to the work of Lacan but concerning ideas with which Lyotard is more in agreement.

Lacan, extending notions drawn from Freud's account of the Oedipus Complex, argues that the loss of the mother constitutes a trauma from which the child never fully recovers – a loss which compounds a series of alienations and separations which increasingly define and divide its subjectivity. The child's acquisition of language (and thus of signs which thereafter mediate its needs in a process Lacan calls 'castration') marks the moment when it can no longer entertain a sense that it enjoys a special access to or unity with the mother (an anxiety already prefigured in its increasing attempts to understand her desires so as to ensure her continued love). The loss of this primal 'object' – which Lacan drawing upon Freud initially refers to as 'the Thing' (*das Ding*) and later *objet a*, and the full significance of which is generated retroactively – provides the constitutive basis for desire that Lacan infamously defines as a 'lack'. That is, that we want what we believe we do not have or is absent because we feel that it will somehow complete us. This lack, around which desire circles thereafter, will haunt the individual throughout his or her life, structuring all of their subsequent or derivative goals and pursuits. They will attempt to paper over or fill this 'hole' in their being, produced as a result of this traumatic loss, by seeking a satisfying substitute (a lover, a job, a car, etc.). However, no object will ever be able to replace the mother (or least what she meant to the child) and thus, for Lacan, the human subject becomes defined and delimited by the endlessly deferred fulfilment of its desire – an indefinite, endless and ultimately futile search for an elusive 'completion'. More importantly, for our purposes, it is clearly evident that Lacan's account turns desire into a by-product of signifying processes: desire is fundamentally internal to and structured by the workings of signifiers (language). It has nothing to do with primary processes, libido, etc.

Lyotard accepts certain aspects of this account. He agrees (subject to certain provisos that we cannot explore here) that the loss of the mother is traumatic and also agrees that the acquisition of language marks a certain type of symbolic 'castration' (denoting accession to the social realm) but from his perspective this still does not refute Freud's account of libido and the primary processes. Certainly, the loss of the mother marks a sense of 'incompletion' which compels the individual into a search for unity and totalisation, and discourse provides a means by which this loss can be provisionally structured and addressed through interaction with others. However, this 'absence' does not ultimately constrain or define how the primary processes work. Language is a structure that is assembled around this gap (as a coping mechanism) but desire does not *arise* from this structure – it is *prior* to it and thus not a 'lack'. Similarly, libido in its movements is largely at odds with the demands of the language structure that dominates secondary processes, despite being subject in part to its constraints.

Where this issue of desire as 'lack' becomes significant, however, and relates back to important aspects of my earlier discussion, is in respect to the way that desire as 'wish' (as the seeking of a phantasmatic substitute or wish-fulfilment) provides material for unconscious transformation. This returns us to Lyotard's account of the ambivalence of desire. The figure-matrix (the existence of which we can infer from the insistence of its effects) is the container through which a certain amount of libido is channelled. I say 'container' with some trepidation because it has no form or location as such – this is merely a metaphorical way of speaking of something 'indeterminate' and thus we should not ascribe to it some mistaken sense of it being an 'unconscious' repository – and certainly not one that is directly reflected in the content which it transforms. To do so would be to fall into the trap of confusing it with what it enables, to put one of the phantasies it produces in its place. Moreover, it does not constitute an origin in the sense that we can speak of an actual, although 'repressed', memory (the primal scene). However, the matrix does provide the conditions for the production of phantasies through which the subject seeks solace or wish-fulfilments in order to counteract a perceived 'loss' or absence. These phantasies involve stagings (the matrix), the production of a hallucinatory or fictional space or scenario (a form) populated with actors, props and actions of a sort (figure). But these same productions will be subject to the indifferent push and pull of desire as a libidinal force – movements which do not respect continuity, logic, consistency, temporality, spatiality, stability or coherence, and which simultaneously figure and disfigure discourses, designations and representations, discourse and perception, concept and image. This energy undoes and disfigures these matrixial productions at the same time that they are born.

This raises the intriguing question of whether art can offer us something different from dreams, or phantasies in general, and the answer turns, quite literally, on Lyotard's account of an anamorphic 'double reversal', or sometimes as he more simply refers to it, the 'rotation' or 'turning inside out'. This notion, derived in part from the writings of the psychoanalyst André

Green, is ultimately perhaps the most important contribution of *Discourse, Figure* because it enables us finally to establish a critical difference between dreams and art. Dreams enact a first reversal or rotation through the operations of the dream-work. This reversal is the 'working over' of material derived from consciousness and the pre-conscious so that words and images no longer signify or designate in their original forms. However, despite these transformations, the dream is still primarily geared towards satisfying a wish-fulfilment. Desire as wish strives to turn and capture desire as libido-force in the pursuit of consolation for a loss or a reconciliation of wish and reality, and as a result the operations of the dream-work become hidden or obscured within its phantasmatic staging (irrespective of the degree of the latter's seeming coherence or lack of it).

Art (or at least art worthy of the name), Lyotard argues, can potentially introduce a second reversal into this process by enacting a further transformation able to turn the entire process around so as to reveal its inner workings. This produces a critical move in which the phantasmatic staging is not fully enacted and thus the wish cannot be fulfilled (even in a compromised form) but is instead deconstructed by exposing the operations that produce the phantasmatic scenario (or underlying wish) as a by-product of the workings of desire.

Lyotard provides a helpful example of what he has in mind here. He describes how the artist Paul Klee mentions in his notebooks how he would sometimes begin drawing, and then after a while would turn the sheet of paper sideways or upside down so that what he saw was no longer recognisable but merely raw material to continue drawing with, and then later he would rotate the sheet back to its original position and continue working it over (DF 226). Although the example describes a literal act of rotation, Lyotard uses it to describe the spirit of what occurs: namely, that Klee overcomes his servitude to wish-fulfilment, notions of intention, and his attachment to semblance or familiarity, through aleatory or trangressive moves that introduce a certain indetermination in to the process and a de-familiarisation of the finished product. This provides a general insight into the workings of avant-garde art (such as 'abstract expressionism') that utilises processes of condensation and displacement, among others, to resist the imposition of recognisable or satisfying forms.

The basic idea here is that unlike the dream which simply works over the 'dream-thoughts' whilst hiding the conditions of its construction (the staging of the wish), an artist can turn these operations around once again so that they then work against themselves and what they produce, thus negating the 'unity' of the finished work through a deconstruction of what has been (re-)presented. Through this 'critical' double reversal the artist produces either one or both of two important effects that Lyotard associates with the figural as transgression: i) that it exposes the workings of the phantasy by foregrounding the mechanism of its construction, and ii) that in doing so it can frustrate the hallucinatory solace promised by the wish-fulfilment. Here critique takes place at the level of form – or more precisely, a deformation or disfiguring is introduced which works specifically against the phantasy, refusing both the seduction of its content and the integration of its elements within a wish-fulfilment.

Lyotard notes, however, that such a critical reversal is not guaranteed in the production and reproduction of artworks. Just as the numerous transformations enacted in the dream-work present no surety that the dream will not finally support or consolidate the substitutive phantasy or wish-fulfilment, so too there is no guarantee that an artwork does not remain complicit with, or even strive to fulfil the phantasy scenario from which it arises (thus disqualifying it as art in Lyotard's sense). Indeed, Lyotard argues that the emergence of recognisable styles, schools and movements in art usually serve to reproduce or preserve the phantasmatic matrix underlying the wish-fulfilment. True artists, for Lyotard, are those who can successfully introduce a further turn or rotation into this process. Refusing to accept a convenient outcome or to automatically reproduce similar works (in terms of a repetitive theme or style) they introduce yet further figural transformations which instead of producing and reinforcing phantasy, or producing a recognisable object or scenario, strive to undo these and foreground their seductive workings.

This finally returns us to the last of the four claims posed at the start of this chapter which will also be taken up again in the next: that *Discourse, Figure* is a supposed detour in pursuit of the 'practical critique of ideology'. It is both a 'detour' and 'practical' because ideological critique necessarily involves showing how ideology, which both shapes and reflects dominant beliefs, values and customs, serves as a means of harnessing individual desire in broader social and political forms. Most types of cultural production present socially licensed phantasies that fulfil a similar function to dreams: that is, the turning of emotionally charged materials into a form that can provide a recognisable and satisfying or socially acceptable outcome. These phantasies, in concert with ideology, seduce people into accepting and conforming to the existing dominant conditions of their society, and serve to ensure that desires are regulated and reconciled with(in) existing social structures and institutions – thus they help maintain the status quo by both short-circuiting the exploration of other social or political possibilities, and redirecting libido into consoling forms of commodification and consumption.

Discourse, Figure was Lyotard's attempt at both laying the groundwork for a critique of how desire becomes captured within and subordinated to these ideological structures and their organisation of social formations, and of creating provisional tools for exposing and deconstructing how phantasies often work within and contribute to sustaining dominant forms of representation. As we will see in the next chapter it is a project that never reached fruition.

Chapter 2

The libidinal

We want structures that serve people, not people serving structures.

Take your desires for reality.

Examples of May 1968 graffiti

We deliver no message, we bear no truth, bring no revelation, and we do not speak for those who remain silent.

Lyotard

While we talk, the sun is getting older.

Lyotard

This chapter provides an overview of Lyotard's philosophy of the late 1960s through to the mid-1970s, retracing and exploring the ideas and themes concerning the libidinal through which it was framed. It also examines the political and intellectual context for the issues and concepts introduced in *Discourse, Figure* and related essays from this period, before turning towards examining ideas detailed in *Libidinal Economy*.

Lyotard's efforts throughout this decade of thinking and writing mark an intense period of 'working through' – of rethinking, resituating, and sometimes even simply abandoning – a number of political and philosophical precepts to which he had previously subscribed. Indeed, he refers to his thinking during this time as one of 'drifting' (in the sense of being adrift upon the ocean), characterised by his movement away from Marxist theory and subsequent traversal of various Freudian concepts.

In respect of Marxist theory this drift had actually begun much earlier in Algeria in the late 1950s, where his investigations and written reports for the journal of the Marxist organisation *Socialisme ou Barbarie* ('Socialism or Barbarism') provided Lyotard with a first-hand and often confronting perspective on the complexities of the plight of the working class and the problems inherent in the Algerian push for independence. These experiences increasingly led him to question the viability of Marxist analyses of, and interventions within, concrete political situations. By the mid-1960s this dissatisfaction with the inadequacies of orthodox Marxist theory and traditional strategies of political engagement led to his break with militant activism and initiated a period of intense personal and political reflection.

Yet, despite this withdrawal from militant activity, Lyotard remained attentive to political developments both in Europe and around the world. The period from 1965 to 1968 saw the emergence of numerous political crises and problems that suggested a turning point was being reached in global affairs. These crises included the efforts of the Soviet Union to suppress dissent within the Warsaw Pact, growing international criticism of American involvement in the Vietnam War, and a variety of protests throughout Europe and the USA concerning issues such as civil liberties, nuclear weapons, the environment, and so forth. More specifically, the Paris riots in May 1968 marked a watershed moment for Lyotard as he became directly involved in the protest movement without recourse to the Marxist organisation that had legitimated and structured his earlier political commitments. The events of May 1968 arose initially from student demonstrations against draconian university policies and a heavy-handed police response but quickly escalated into mass strikes and protests by various groups across France in support of the students' demands. These actions temporarily paralysed the workings of industry and government, and led to barricades being assembled from cars and detritus found in the streets of Paris, and pitched battle between protestors and riot police.

Many onlookers believed that France teetered on the brink of civil war, whilst others foresaw the possibility of a new revolution. Few, however, doubted that something fundamental and historically significant was occurring – an event marked by an intense dissatisfaction and frustration that temporarily united disparate and otherwise incompatible groups in a common, if somewhat nebulous, cause. Indeed, many French intellectuals felt initially energised by this unforeseen turn of events, feeling a revolutionary zeal and optimism, and believing that it portended enormous imminent social change, but were subsequently disappointed and enervated by how quickly this potential seemed to dissipate in the face of various 'betrayals' (e.g. of the communist party which sided with the government, and the opportunism of trade unions which used the situation as leverage for higher wages) that marked the beginnings of a conservative political and social backlash.

It was within the context of these social and political upheavals and antagonisms – the promise of things unprecedented and the disappointment resulting from their seeming failure – and the intense, passionate outpouring of emotions that accompanied them, that Lyotard found himself confronted by the limitations of his earlier views, of unsuccessfully attempting to contain such events within traditional party rhetoric and explanatory models concerning class dynamics or the 'dialectical movement of history'. These political situations revealed themselves to be far more complex in reality than they had previously appeared in theory: shouting revolutionary slogans no more made one a radical agent of change than waiting to cross at the traffic lights necessarily made you a dupe of authority; nor did employment in a factory necessarily ensure the presence of a politicised consciousness, any more than working in a university automatically made one a compliant state functionary.

In short, the diversity of such varied and competing demands, fears and expectations suggested that the social systems, institutions and conventional theoretical explanations of the time were inadequate to account for what was taking place. As a result, Lyotard began to look elsewhere for answers, feeling that somehow these issues were tied to the movements of desire, of individuals' and groups' wishes and phantasies, of what they both consciously and unconsciously believed and felt – that is, the realities that they had constructed in their own minds – and how specific institutions within and social formations more broadly, responded to, manipulated and regulated these same desires.

In a series of essays and interviews collected and reprinted in the first edition of *Dérive à partir de Marx et Freud* (several of which are translated in *Driftworks*), dating from 1968 up to and including the publication of *Discourse, Figure*, Lyotard foregrounds his own doubts whilst still presenting a relatively consistent political perspective. In these articles he still avows some kind of relationship to Marxist notions of alienation, ideology and critique (albeit subject to increasing revision). It is worth briefly examining these notions before proceeding further as they provide a revealing contrast for some of the internal mutations that libidinal philosophy undergoes. Clear presentations of these views are outlined in several of the interviews and essays (see particularly 'On Theory' and 'On the Critical Function of the Work of Art' in *Driftworks*) where, despite his break with militant Marxism, Lyotard affirms his commitment to the necessity and value of theoretical analysis, declaring that the 'function of theory is not only to understand, but also to criticize, i.e. to call into question and overturn a reality…it must consist in the overturning of a mystified or alienated reality' (DW19).

Lyotard describes the purpose of such critique as primarily one of ideological 'demystification', of exposing the links between the general condition of social alienation under capitalism – which he defines as 'the experiencing of a false, abstract universality…[consisting,] for example, in the fact that anything can be exchanged for anything else through the mediation of money' (DW 20–1) – and the representational forms through which mystification is achieved and maintained.

Noticeably, the notion of ideology here still retains a privileged role, subject to certain revisions. In Marx and Engels' account of ideology they likened its workings, the dissemination and promotion of the ideas, values and self-justifications of the ruling class, to a camera obscura – an optical device used by artists, containing a mirror that inverts the observed image – in which the subordinate groups in society uncritically take on board these ideas despite their incompatibility with their own economic and political disempowerment. In doing so the oppressed unwittingly view their world in an analogous 'upside-down' manner. The key idea is that individuals in capitalist society misconceive their own relation to their labour, to themselves, to others, and to their environment more broadly, thus giving them a distorted view – or 'false consciousness' – of how society functions that obscures or veils the real or true dynamics underlying economic, social and political inequity.

Lyotard reconfigures this notion. Whereas for Marx and his followers the 'overturning' of ideology would thereafter reveal the true state of things (thus implying that there was an objective reality or truth beyond or apart from ideology all along, the identification of which would be a key step in enabling social transformation and the overcoming of alienation), Lyotard is less inclined to accept such a straightforward and simplistic notion of an objective, unmediated reality. Instead he shifts the emphasis towards what he calls 'demystification' in which the aim is to expose how cultural representations are complicit with the perpetuation of the status quo, without committing to either a notion of what such an independent reality would be, or to a social or political programme denoting what changes and outcomes would be required thereafter. Thus the aim of critique is not to reveal the underlying 'truth', but rather to expose the construction of the ongoing lie – the phantasy that leads people to believe that there is in fact a definitive truth or answer awaiting them.

The main preoccupation of Lyotard in these interviews and articles is no longer political analysis in the traditional sense, as referring to political parties, economic analyses and social agendas (i.e. the sorts of activities that he had undertaken during the Algerian situation), but of analysing the place or role of art within the latter half of the twentieth century, a role which he re-conceives in both ontological and critical terms (i.e. concerning the way we live and how we evaluate how we live). In this perspective, Lyotard sees art as having supplanted politics as the primary resistant and critical space within which new perspectives on old problems can be foregrounded. However, he argues that in doing so art neither illustrates these problems nor presents solutions to them, but by its very presence, its potentially unassimilable intransigence, it initiates a questioning of the status quo and all that this entails. Moreover, it is to the form and not the content of art that Lyotard looks for its radical potential.

In order to fully grasp what Lyotard intends it is worth briefly examining his claim that art in the twentieth century performs a different role or function from its previous historical incarnations. In earlier societies the representational forms and phenomena that today we usually group under the name of 'art' (keeping in mind that the very category of 'art' that we employ, strictly speaking, did not exist as such in very ancient societies, where cultural forms were not usually seen as separate from daily life or distinct from matters of ritual or worship) were primarily religious in nature and function. They had both a sacred or spiritual role and an integrative function: that is, they were a key means of communion, of thus binding communities and providing them with a shared basis of communication (DW 71).

The representations of these sets of beliefs and 'rhythmic' – that is, seasonally oriented and therefore cyclical – rituals that these societies used to make sense of themselves, provided the 'organic' bonds that held them together, providing some sense of social unity or harmony (DW 27). In an important sense, art's primary function in such societies was the maintenance of the social, spiritual, economic and political status quo, and thus of constraining and mediating change. It had no real significance or existence or justification apart from this. Moreover, this function was closely linked to the creation and maintenance of easily identifiable means for ensuring shared social and cultural identities, for 'it created good forms, some sort of a myth, of a ritual, a rhythm, a medium other than language through which the members of a society would communicate by participating… [i]n a common substratum of meaning' (DW 27).

Immediately thereafter Lyotard declares: 'This has now become impossible'! He claims that the historical development of capitalism in the West, and the experience of modernity more broadly – as a break with, and a shattering of, traditional social forms and institutions and ways of living and thinking – has produced irreversible social, economic and political transformations in which these earlier conditions can no longer be sustained, revived or reinstated. This type of overt and all-embracing religious, social structure no longer has any functional validity and is thus permanently inaccessible, despite the ongoing mourning and eulogies for its loss that pervade much of contemporary culture, such as the nostalgic (and phantasmatic) calls for a return to traditional 'values' or 'truth', of getting back to 'nature', or of a return to a simpler, non-materialistic lifestyle.

Lyotard argues that the constitutive social alienation of capitalism, and the corresponding differentiation, fragmentation and specialisation of labour that resulted in the identification and categorisation of the artist (or artisan) as someone characterised by a marketable set of technical skills, finally leads in the early twentieth century to the marginalisation of art from the social mainstream. More importantly, it results in the congruent separation of certain artists' efforts and products from any specific given social function – indeed, from any identifiable function at all.

He claims that this new-found indeterminate status, which characterises the avant-garde of the early twentieth century and those still committed to its legacy, situates the artist (and the artwork as the product of the artist's 'labours') in a potentially unique position. They are now able to examine critically and expose such nostalgic hankerings for a 'lost' sense of community – not simply the earlier myths of organic bonds but also both the more narcissistic and revolutionary phantasies that have taken their place within contemporary capitalist and 'socialist' societies – as well as the prevalent phantasies that provide the illusion or promise of social harmony: 'The function of the artist...is no longer to produce good forms, new good forms, but on the contrary to deconstruct them systematically and accelerate their obsolescence. And this indefinitely, by attacking them on all levels.' (DW 26)

This is made possible because of the (potential) change in the significance of art itself as a form of practice. No longer necessarily bound by economic, religious or political demands or expectations, art (or at least avant-garde art) has the potential to question every aspect of contemporary life, including its own meaning, status and purpose, and thus to help us confront, explore, and live with the inherent uncertainty of modern existence without resorting to simplistic reassurances or authoritative (and authoritarian) political or social structures. That the majority of what is usually called art today demonstrates little awareness of this potential, let alone any inclination to pursue it, is an issue that I will return to in later chapters.

A key part of Lyotard's argument is his belief that artists must, on the one hand, resist calls for a renewal of art's 'relevance' and social utility and, on the other, relinquish any aim or desire of uniting or integrating the fragmented and alienated components of society, of providing solace or restoring the organic unity that characterised traditional communities – for not only are these demands and aspirations obsolete but also impossible to meet. In respect to the first, art faces a number of competing but impossible demands, when it is not simply dismissed as a bourgeois indulgence, or a form of distracting entertainment, an elitist pretension, or of little practical value. Various groups insist that it somehow demonstrate its relevance or usefulness: by providing or advocating ideals of social harmony, or directly depicting and thus exposing social inequities, or showing what needs to be done to fix them, or lifting the community's spirits, or by civilising the more wild or unruly areas of society. All of these demands collectively strive to subordinate art to various agendas for change or to programs for social engineering that are at odds, Lyotard claims, with art's own indeterminate nature.

Instead, avant-garde art, through its irreconcilability with these aims, exposes the latter's 'ideological' and mystifying underpinnings: how they invoke imaginary bonds that seduce or contain the individual within the existing social fabric or framework. This process of scrutiny and exposure is what Lyotard means by 'critique'. And indeed, the history and appeals of 'revolutionary' action are not exempt from its questioning, with invocations of utopian programs and manifestos no less ideological in this sense than the social formations or inequities or beliefs they claim to overcome.

This necessary incapacity of art to predict or promise a specific outcome renders the notion of 'political art' or 'revolutionary art' (i.e. an art that depicts or promotes social reform or a social revolution in the pursuit of a specific goal) self-contradictory, even nonsensical. To aspire to provide such content is to fall into the trap of positioning art as something that can reconcile, or contribute to the healing of, a divided society. The inevitable result of this delusion is not the production of revolutionary art but rather a prescriptive propaganda. Obvious examples would be Soviet-style 'socialist realism' of the kind promoted by Andrei Zhdanov, with its infantile and delusional depictions of heroic workers wielding tools or happy socialists driving tractors in the name of the revolution, or the Nazis' pernicious glorification of racial purity and dismissal of modernism as degenerate, or even their respective celebration of the personality cults of Stalin and Hitler. Each of these phantasies whilst promising leadership, truth, purity or utopia, instead manipulatively masqueraded as art, and any deviations from the party line on what constituted appropriate content and style were punished or liquidated.

In an important sense, however, such propaganda is not the perversion of 'political art' but its inevitable fulfilment, for art, according to Lyotard, has no political goals or social answers apart from questioning the recognisable status quo (and even the questions it poses are not necessarily comprehensible). Indeed, art that questions and deconstructs is, for Lyotard, revolutionary by definition. It has no pre-given object or objective, no aim or goal in itself, apart from transgressing or resisting the social givens:

> [as this] deconstructing activity is a truly radical critical activity for it does not deal with the *signifieds* of things, but with their plastic organisation, their signifying organisation. It shows that the problem is not so much of knowing what a given discourse says, but rather how it is disposed...that the deconstruction of its disposition is going to reveal its mystifying content. (DW 29)

Art does not, and cannot, show the way forward. It cannot depict such a goal, a utopia, without necessarily betraying it in advance – and in this sense, the term 'avant-garde' is misleading and, as Lyotard admits, not very appropriate or well suited as a descriptor, although for historical reasons it is the term that we are stuck with. As soon as art purports to provide any kind of definitive answer it turns into a phantasmatic wish-fulfilment, or ideology, of the kind that it otherwise exposes or thwarts.

However, just as art faces the threat of its appropriation as political propaganda so too does it face the equally threatening (and far more common) prospect of its assimilation and commodification by capitalism. This colonisation of artists' efforts, the reduction of their works to forms of cultural or economic capital and the appropriation of their ideas and techniques within the marketplace of manipulative advertising, compels the avant-garde to seek escape from such encroachments in a movement that is simultaneously both a flight away from capitalism and a movement towards other as yet unforeseen possibilities (DW 32).

Lyotard freely acknowledges that this process in which art both exposes and frustrates the seductive workings of ideology (demystifying attempts at the construction of a pseudo-religion) whilst being under the continuous threat of assimilation, renders its critical and deconstructive efforts interminable – at least given society's almost inexhaustible capacity for self-delusion and craving for wish-fulfilment. It is only in this sense, he adds, that we can speak in terms of 'permanent revolution' – of something, which although capable of interruption or cessation, is without end (if by an 'end' we mean a pre-determined goal or inherent notion of completion).

It is within the context of these views that *Discourse, Figure* is positioned as a 'detour' intended to provide the (self-reflexive) theoretical groundwork for taking the insights derived from the deconstructive activity of avant-garde art – the notions of the figural and the 'double reversal' discussed in the previous chapter – and applying them to ideological solicitation, that is the construction and manipulation of social phantasies (of wish-fulfilment) that sustain and perpetuate the status quo. By making a philosophy of 'desire' and its workings the basis for such a critique, Lyotard hoped to provide a means of intervening directly in the political and social sphere without falling into the trap of proffering any kind of determinate political manifesto or social agenda for change.

Yet, despite Lyotard's detailed development of this detour the actual project of a practical critique of ideology never subsequently took place. Instead his increasing pursuit of the notion of the libidinal forced a rethinking of his own commitment to, and the usefulness of, some of the ideas of this 'transitional' period. In the wake of the publication of *Discourse, Figure*, from approximately 1972 until late 1974, Lyotard began to develop and expand the libidinal aspects of this perspective to the detriment of the earlier 'residual' Marxist concepts. Indeed, such notions as alienation, ideology and critique were gradually modified or relinquished in favour of new concepts less seemingly entangled in the inherent problems of traditional political and cultural analysis.

We have already noted that Lyotard's embrace of the libidinal was in part a response to the political crises of the mid to late 1960s and the subsequent search for new terms and concepts for political analysis, but the intellectual context for these transformations was just as crucial a catalyst, because it was to philosophy and the various innovations by, and within, psychoanalysis, anthropology, sociology, psychology, and communications theory that he looked for new ways of thinking. Arguably, there were two significant intellectual influences on Lyotard during this period: Lacan and Deleuze.

On returning to Paris after leaving Algeria, Lyotard had begun attending Jacques Lacan's psychoanalytic seminars whilst writing his doctoral dissertation, the latter being in many ways a working through of his various disagreements with and revisions of Lacan's ideas, as well as broader issues related to developments in semiotics and structuralism that intersected with Lacan's theories. As *Discourse, Figure* makes clear Lyotard was highly critical of these three approaches, particularly their claims or aspirations to being both scientific and comprehensive. Moreover, his own study of phenomenology and his political experiences had left him highly sceptical of the all-embracing 'linguistic turn' and obsession with the 'structure of signification' on which Lacanian psychoanalysis, semiotics and structuralism (and other theories influenced by them) were principally founded, leading him to say at the time – with one eye on the influence of Saussurean linguistics and perhaps the other on the rising fortunes of Derrida – that 'one does not at all break with metaphysics by putting language everywhere' (DF 14). However, the value of Lacan's seminar for Lyotard was its foregrounding of the notion of desire, and its suggestion (linguistic structures aside) that desire's workings were 'trans-subjective': that these unconscious processes were as much social as individual.

The second key influence on Lyotard's ideas and approach to the libidinal was the work of Gilles Deleuze. Throughout the 1960s, Deleuze had been slowly but methodically producing and analysing a 'lineage' of philosophers, artists and writers – including Bergson, Spinoza, Freud, Proust – whose works engaged with the problem of difference and its subordination to principles of identity and opposition. This led him to write two extremely important and generally influential philosophical works which also significantly impacted on Lyotard: the first was a groundbreaking analysis of Nietzsche's thought and the second Deleuze's doctoral thesis, *Difference and Repetition*.

Similarly shaken by the events of May 1968, and increasingly critical of the work of Lacan, Deleuze had begun, in the aftermath of the Paris riots, to develop his own version of a 'philosophy of desire', in collaboration with Guattari, an ex-communist psychoanalyst and former student of Lacan's, who with Jean Oury ran the experimental psychiatric clinic at La Borde. Motivated by similar concerns to Lyotard, and partly influenced by ideas promoted in his *Discourse, Figure*, Deleuze and Guattari's detailing of a philosophy of desire was finally published in 1972. This book, *Anti-Oedipus*, the first part of a proposed two-volume project called 'Capitalism and Schizophrenia', was quickly taken up (and largely misunderstood) by the media as a scandalous and wholesale assault on the ideas of Freud and Lacan and the institution of psychoanalysis in general. Significantly, the publication of *Anti-Oedipus* and several related articles led Lyotard, in turn, to rethink some of his own ideas concerning Freud and the libidinal, resulting two years later in the publication of his own mature elaboration of a philosophy of desire, *Libidinal Economy* (1974).

If there is one fundamental common idea or premise underlying and uniting both Lyotard and Deleuze and Guattari's respective projects it is the overt linking of desire to politics – or rather the re-conceptualisation of politics in terms of desire and its workings. This is not to suggest that such attempts were unprecedented – the application of psychoanalytic concepts in understanding political and social structures and behaviours was hardly new, already being implicit within Freud's own later writings, and of course, Lacan's subsequent reworking of Freud. Similarly, attempts at specifically fusing Marxist and Freudian concepts had several notable precursors, beginning with the work of Wilhelm Reich in the 1920s and 1930s, followed by the efforts of Adorno and Horkheimer in the 1940s and 1950s, and the writings of Marcuse and also Althusser in the 1960s.

What distinguishes the respective efforts of Lyotard and of Deleuze and Guattari, however, from earlier attempts at a synthesis of Marx and Freud is their preparedness, unlike their predecessors, to place more emphasis upon the contributions of psychoanalytic theory (subject to several major criticisms and revisions) than on traditional Marxist concepts and analysis, *and* to premise their own analysis on the axiom of an energetic 'substrate' common to both the social and the individual – thus making the notion of libido the focus and linchpin of their respective theories.

Lyotard and Deleuze and Guattari were not the first to note the parallel between a Marxist notion of labour-power as a fluid and energetic social flow that provides the basis for capitalist investment and Freud's account of the polymorphous mobility and potential cathexes (investments) of libido. However, they were among the first to develop this insight in detail, and to no longer view it in terms of an analogy drawn between the two types of flow but of revealing instead that they are literally different yet related aspects of the same differentiating force (i.e. desire) expressed or manifested at two different levels. In doing so, they posit the economic and political organisation of society and the 'psyches' of its constituent members as two closely related articulations and distributions of desire at work in the world. From this perspective the libidinal always constitutes and functions as part of an economy and this economy is always already political. Indeed, as Lyotard points out, neither Freud nor Marx's theories were ever offered up as theories of meaning (that is, in respect of the content of capitalism or the psyche) but instead were attempts to account for how meaning and value were actually produced (in terms of their form and function).

Lyotard's subsequent development of this idea in his own writings demonstrates a highly selective use of Freud's theories as regards which concepts were retained, revised or abandoned. For example, Lyotard favours the earlier topographical model of the workings of the psyche (consciousness, preconscious and unconscious) over the later structural model (id, ego and superego). He also displays no interest whatsoever in the clinical or therapeutic application (at least in any conventional sense) of psychoanalytic concepts. More significantly, given his interest in art, Lyotard rejects Freud's own readings of artworks with their clumsy appeals to symbolism and obsession with decoding content (indicating that Freud did not fully grasp the implications of his own insights in his analysis of the 'dream-work').

Similarly Lyotard rejected Freud's related notions of 'psychopathography' and 'sublimation' as either comprehensive or even convincing explanations of creativity and art. In respect to the first, he rejects as reductive and misguided such diagnostic 'readings' of artworks as 'symptoms', an approach which interprets them in terms of artists' personalities, illnesses or subconscious fears, and as direct reflections of the psychic state or inadequacy of the individual artist and the events of the artist's life. In respect to the second, sublimation (i.e. the notion that art stems primarily from the displacement or channelling of unacceptable aggressive or sexual impulses into socially acceptable forms, thus representing a reconciliation between the artist's own psyche and the needs of society), he argues that art has an expressive and ontological relation to libido but need not serve any mediating social function.

Lyotard claims that art, by invoking a transgressive 'figural' otherness, challenges and works against such phantasies of reconciliation, unravelling the ambitions and satisfactions of a subjectivity that strives to assert mastery over itself and its environment or to reach a rapprochement between them. He suggests that Freud's reading of artworks in terms of the artist's psychic life and of the sublimating of his or her basic impulses arises from, on the one hand, Freud's own theoretical indecisiveness about whether desire is a force (and one that is indifferent to what it invests) *or* a form of wish-fulfilment, and, on the other hand, Freud's conservative and reactionary aesthetics. Freud's 'classical' education had left him completely uninterested in (even hostile to) the revolution in art that was occurring around him at the time that he was writing. Indeed, his famous brief encounter with his Surrealist admirer, André Breton, in which Freud found the latter's views on the unconscious and politics to be completely incomprehensible, demonstrates Freud's deep-seated antipathy towards avant-garde art or its radical potential.

As we have already seen, Freud's notions of desire, libido and the primary processes provided Lyotard in *Discourse, Figure* with the means for constructing a flexible perspective from which to engage and refute these reactionary notions concerning art. In particular the notion of 'double reversal' presented a critical technique for deconstructing social phantasies through an intervention at the level of form. However, thereafter Lyotard began to develop the implications of the libidinal in ways that increasingly questioned several of the theoretical concepts underlying this earlier view. Much of this revision stems from the fact that Lyotard grants the notion of libido far greater significance than did Freud himself. Whereas for the latter, libido which, as the fundamental energy characteristic of the psyche could be invested in or attached to various ideas, perceptions and representations, was but one part of his theory, Lyotard now makes it the focus of everything. It becomes a universal and endlessly malleable force without any identity of its own, but from which everything else derives. This shifts the orientation of Lyotard's research towards exploring the implications of this change, raising new related questions concerning how libido, which as the characteristic energy of the primary processes and thus supposedly positive in nature, can manifest as, and produce, negative effects.

An important innovation within libidinal philosophy that enables Lyotard to address this question is his introduction of the notion of the 'dispositif' (a difficult term to translate, as in French it can mean a 'set-up' or apparatus or assemblage in a mechanical or physical sense, as well as suggesting a more organic disposition or habit or way of being). Lyotard defines the dispositif as the structure or set-up through which libido is distributed, channelled, sluiced, dammed and stored. It is essentially a form of organisation that regulates the flow and distribution of libidinal energy.

There are many different such dispositifs and they can take numerous different forms. Lyotard suggests that any and all aspects of social reality can be (and are) related to or appropriated into such dispositifs or assemblages (the general description of which bears some resemblance to Deleuze and Guattari's own notion of 'desiring-machines'). The bringing into contact of various things or surfaces through such a dispositif enables an exchange of energy. For example, energy is transferred just as much by, and across, signs, ideas and feelings, as through bodies and machines. Whether it involves raising one's voice, kissing a lover, stroking a cat, painting a picture, watching a film, driving a car, presenting a theory, mocking authority, telling a story, putting on a play or throwing a rock, all such activities involve the transfer of libidinal energy from one point to another, from one place to another (either within or across the body or between bodies). However, as we shall see, it is the question of whether the movement of this energy across these constituent parts (and the effects it produces) is free, constrained or curtailed that becomes the crucial issue, the political crux, for Lyotard.

One of the most interesting and powerful examples of a libidinal dispositif that Lyotard provides (and which builds upon *Discourse, Figure*'s notion of phantasy and its structure and support) is what he names the 'theatrical model of representation', the staging and splitting of desire, which he claims is the dominant form of representation in Western culture, and the form most complicit with the way that authority is legitimated and power is controlled and distributed. This model denotes a structure through which desire is shaped and directed in respect to a 'lack', and thus constitutes a mechanism that channels and regulates libidinal energy, dis-intensifying or dampening and redirecting affect into particular social and political forms.

Lyotard's description and analysis of this model is first introduced in the article 'Painting as a Libidinal Set-up', and developed in various related works including 'On a Figure of Discourse', 'Beyond Representation', 'The Tooth, The Palm', 'Several Silences', *Libidinal Economy* and (subject to certain revisions) his 1977 article 'The Unconscious as Mise en Scène'.

In 'Painting as a Libidinal Set-up' (1973) Lyotard presents the schematic of a typical theatre or performance venue consisting of divisions or boundaries that delimit or separate, whilst simultaneously relating, several different 'spaces'. First, there is the building or enclosure (see boundary 1 in Figure 4) that separates the internal spaces from the world or supposed reality

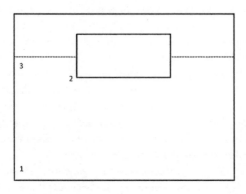

4. Diagram of theatrical representation.

– thus dividing an 'inside' from an 'outside' or exterior. Within the theatre itself, at its centre, is the 'stage' or performing area (boundary 2) often demarcated by a difference in elevation, or a particular shape, or surrounding empty space, or footlights, or a definitive border or frame, or some combination thereof. The stage is divided in turn from two other spaces, the first being the auditorium where the audience sits or stands in a usually immobilised or constrained fashion, and the second is distinguished by a less visible but more significant boundary (3). This last limit sets apart the backstage area or the wings (which can also include lighting rigs on the ceiling, underground storage or machinery, orchestra pits, a bio-box or projectionist's booth, etc.) that provide the *support* for what is staged or seen but which in and of itself remains beyond view: 'We have to put all the scenography behind this limit. *All that effaces and is effaced, hides and is hidden at the same time*' (LRAG 321).

Certain implications follow from these divisions. First, what is inside this enclosure is granted a certain status, constituting a phantasmatic space of representation, the value of which is completely relative to, or determined by, what is external to it, to what it seeks to represent or stand in place of. Lyotard is not just referring to what is on the stage here but quite literally everything inside the space produced by the first limit.

Secondly, this is a space shaped not by simulation or deception but seduction. Although it is a phantasmatic space that produces or solicits particular affects or meanings in the audience, the latter do not directly confuse what they see in this space with empirical or perceptual reality, anymore than an observer mistakes a *trompe l'oeil* for the scene that it depicts, or an infant visually mistakes its thumb for the mother's nipple. Somehow and at some level the audience comes to accept or welcome the substitutive representation in place of reality because it provides a certain type of pleasure or reassurance (or consolation).

Thirdly, and following on from the second point, the first division is the most politically and socially problematic (for it is the one which experimental theatre, to take the theatrical model literally for a moment, has rarely been able to circumvent) and the one that denotes the nihilism of this model – an important claim that I will return to shortly. Why? Because what is depicted on the stage is supposedly a representation of something outside the theatre – this is why it is a *re*-presentation – thus raising or positioning what is purportedly 'external' to a transcendent or privileged level. What occurs on the stage (the interior) is justified or legitimated according to something that this very space excludes by default (the exterior), and this clearly suggests a 'political' dimension concerning what is represented and how it is represented.

Fourthly, what primarily sustains this process of seduction and transcendence, and in fact, props up the entire model, are the hidden or unseen workings of the support or machinery produced by boundary 3 (the backstage that largely contributes to sustaining the division between inside and outside that *Discourse, Figure* sought to expose).

Lyotard presents various examples across several articles of how this theatrical model, as the construction of something that refers to a meaning external to what is seen, applies and operates in otherwise seemingly disparate domains. In 'Painting as a Libidinal Set-up' the focus is on painting as a form of representation that reflects the general structure of the theatrical model – in this case via the physical and literal frame (boundary 2), the support in the form of paint, canvas, brush technique, stretcher, primer, linear perspective, etc. (boundary 3), and the exhibiting space or gallery (boundary 1). It is important, however, to keep in mind that Lyotard is specifically referring here to 'mimetic' or 'realistic' paintings that strive to depict familiar or recognisable objects and scenes. As will become clearer later, although more abstract or avant-garde works are also dispositifs or set-ups, they do not usually fit within this theatrical model.

Similarly, Lyotard suggests that the construction of a defined and delimited political forum, separated off from broader society, and in which only certain people can presume to speak or act on behalf of authority or the populace in general, presents another version of the theatrical model, and more significantly one in which the workings, and self-authorisations, of power are enacted or performed (whilst the mechanisms that sustain and legitimise these performances remain largely invisible).

Even within conventional psychoanalytic theory we find this same theatricalisation where the unconscious is depicted as a stage, a hollowed-out space within the psyche, or as a separate but more fundamentally determinative structure. The 'fort-da' game mentioned in the previous chapter is an obvious example – the child's cot is a stage where something absent is represented (the mother) and its loss and potential recovery are enacted through the prop or support of a cotton reel and thread. It constitutes a psychic theatre in which Freud and Lacan are no less seduced than Freud's grandchild.

In respect to a more philosophical example it is not difficult to see that Lyotard's description also evokes Plato's famous 'Allegory of the Cave', wherein Plato provides a metaphorical illustration of how each of us is imprisoned within his own perceptions and subjective opinions and is divorced from the truth. The tale recounts how people are imprisoned in a cave, shackled such that they can only see the back wall that they face. Behind the prisoners is a fire and between them and the flames walk strange people carrying various dummies and props. The prisoners, unable to see what is truly taking place, mistake for reality the shadows cast by this scenario on to the back wall that they are facing. They cannot see the true reality that exists outside of the cave. Plato uses this allegory to illustrate how, imprisoned within our own bodies, feelings and prejudices, and subject to social conformity, we pervert the truths obscured by our senses yet revealed by reason.

Lyotard's reference to the theatre-like qualities of the cave (and one should add that numerous commentators have also noted how much its depiction of an image projected before an immobilised audience functions as a precursor to the cinematic apparatus), implicate Plato's philosophy within the perpetuation and legitimation of this dispositif that Lyotard describes as nihilistic. By positing an 'outside' or 'beyond' to experience where truth or reality supposedly resides, Plato provides the model for a way of thinking that has subsequently exerted enormous influence over Western culture.

Before examining the nihilistic aspects of this model let us briefly look at the implications of libidinal organisation. In an essay titled 'Acinema' published in 1973, Lyotard gives a more developed and extensive example of how such a libidinal set-up can work to regulate desire. He begins by noting that cinema consists primarily in the depiction of movements, it is 'the inscription of movement, a writing with movement' at various levels, including 'the film shot, those of the actors and other moving objects, those of lights, colour, frame and lens; in the film sequence, all of these again plus the cuts and splices of editing; for the film as a whole, those of the final script and the spatio-temporal synthesis of the narration' (LR 169). He emphasises this otherwise straightforward observation in order to highlight the fact that film functions as a libidinal economy, as a means of organising and distributing energy (both at the level of the institution of cinema and in respect to any given film), where movement reflects the flows and montages of libidinal investments, the movements of desire. As such, film involves the two competing forms of desire that we mentioned in the last chapter: desire as libido-force and its channelling in the form of desire as wish. However, the institution of film (and here Lyotard means the social, industrial and economic production of mainstream and independent commercial cinema) subordinates the former to the latter, through a filtering process in which only those movements are preserved which reinforce the film as a whole. Only those elements are retained which contribute to its 'good form' (its theatrical representation) and utility in respect to sustaining the social structure in which it exists, because acquiring 'the techniques of film-making involves knowing how to eliminate a large number of these possible movements' such that 'image, sequence and film must be constituted at the price of these exclusions' (LR 169).

These exclusions or effacements concern those supposedly erroneous, deficient or aberrant shots and edits that do not simply distract or detract from the general integrity of the finished product but which, in fact, constitute illegitimate discharges of libidinal energy. These include: shots that contradict the flow of the narrative or are inconsistent with the representational *mise en scène*, shots which are not comprehensible in respect to the surrounding shots, or edits that confuse the viewer, or conflict with the flow of action, and so forth.

The primary criterion for these exclusions is coherence, inasmuch as a mistake is eliminated 'because of its incongruity, and in order to protect the order of the whole...while banning the intensity that it carries' – intensities which otherwise can be co-opted into a regulated and contained form. Thus Lyotard asserts that 'the order of the whole has its sole object in the functioning of the cinema: that there be order in the movements, that the movements be made in order, that they make order...*The so-called impression of reality is a real oppression of orders*' (emphasis added, LR 170).

He argues that there are two competing types of movement at stake here (presumably alluding to George Bataille's notions of 'restricted' and 'general economy', of energy being reinvested in social utility or expended in un-recuperable ways). On the one hand, there is what Lyotard calls the 'enforcement of a nihilism of movement', in which movements are productive but only in the sense that they always give themselves up to a higher purpose or structure in respect to the overall organisation of filmic material, and, on the other, a perverse, '*sterile difference in an audio-visual field*', involving a movement that has no other purpose than to exist in and of itself. The example of the latter that Lyotard offers is of a small child compulsively striking a match so as to watch it briefly flare and consume itself. It is sterile because its incandescence leads nowhere and means nothing (for it is pure expenditure), and the libidinal pleasure that it generates in the child involves nothing more than a random discharge of energy, akin to the match's own conflagration. And it is perverse because it does not produce anything or lend itself to economic interaction, or any recognisable social utility (as libido in typical 'species' sexuality would otherwise analogously lend itself to reproduction and self-preservation). In contrast, conventional filmic structure works to capture and recuperate such energetic investment or discharge in the relationship between the viewer and the integration of filmic images.

Lyotard views this constrained (re-)productivity of the cinematic process as indicative, not just of a schematic model of the reinforcement of social ideologies, but of the general workings of capitalist industry itself. Its workings are analogous – even extensions of – the processes of commodification and associative forms of production that enmesh each of us within a dispositif of ongoing consumption that sustains the entire desiring machinery of the marketplace. Capital as investment initiates a cyclical process of investment and return, and subsequent re-investment of this return, and so on, potentially ad infinitum. Similarly, the pleasures offered up by cinema constitute a form of 'return' in which libido or affect is continually reinvested back into sustaining the economic and social system as it exists, and subordinating it to 'the sacred task of making itself recognisable to the eye'. This organisation of the filmic material involves a subordination of all the elements to the whole such that dissonance is ideally resolved or eliminated: 'All so-called good form implies the return of sameness, the folding back of diversity upon an identical unity...disciplining the movements, limiting them to the norms of tolerance characteristic of the system...' (LR 172–3).

This is not to suggest that seemingly aberrant elements cannot be present in such types of film, but they are only ever permissible on the condition that they function as temporary deferrals, after which they are recuperated at a higher level of meaning, and reintegrated back into the totality (LR 173). For example, the non-linear narratives of films such as *Pulp Fiction* or *Memento*, despite their seeming unconventionality or transgressiveness, do not really escape the dictates of this model, instead merely reinforcing its workings in variant form. In the end, such deviations are simply temporary detours that enhance the meaningful totality of the filmic text's narrative (as is evident from the ease with which they can be reassembled into a linear form).

Perhaps better examples of films that exist on the margins of the 'commercial' sector and which potentially include genuinely aberrant and un-recuperable elements, might include the films of Jean-Luc Godard of the mid to late 1960s, or the improvisational films of John Cassavetes (in which he refused to remove lens flare, overly dark or unfocused shots, objects obscuring actors' faces, etc.), or even several of the films of David Lynch. However, although these might possibly constitute exceptions, they are not the resistant sorts of films that Lyotard really has in mind. From his perspective, commercial (even independent) cinema constitutes a form of 'libidinal normalisation' in which the ideal of integration and systematic self-enclosure of the text corresponds to a similar ideal of social integration and totalisation.

In contrast to this dispositif, Lyotard advocates an 'acinema' in which aleatory or disfiguring elements work to resist the ready assimilation of filmic images into processes of 'visual identification', narrative totalisation, textual comprehension or general commodification. This can take a number of ('bad') forms that share the common trait of foregrounding and distorting or transforming the 'support' (exposing and frustrating the process of producing cinematic meaning or verisimilitude). This can involve shifting the emphasis from the immobility of the support to its mobility, or the exaggerated acceleration or deceleration of movements, or the contraction or protraction of shot duration, or the increased use of fragmentation or abstraction – all with the aim of resisting cohesion and comprehension.

Lyotard gives an excellent illustration of such an a-cinematic filmic assemblage in his article 'The Unconscious as Mise en Scène' where he describes one of the experimental films of Michael Snow, *La Région Centrale*, which involved the attachment of a camera to a specially constructed film apparatus or mechanical set-up. This piece of machinery randomly forced the camera (beginning with an arbitrary starting point and a similarly arbitrary end point) to pass through a number of lateral movements and rotations, in which over a long enough period of time all 360 degrees of the environment could be potentially 'filmed' (including views of the mechanical apparatus itself). However, throughout the process the arbitrariness of the camera's unrelated movements continually works to frustrate the viewer's attempts at constructing (or synthesising from this diversity of 'views') a narrative, or a coherent viewpoint or satisfying conceptual overview, or a sense of unified space (or even a phantasmatic space), by dividing all the possibilities of the visual field into a heterogeneous multiplicity of perspectives that cannot be integrated.

This brief discussion of 'Acinema' in respect to the libidinal dispositif raises another important aspect of the theatrical model that I have held off discussing but which is crucial to its dominance – its nihilistic nature. Taking his lead from Friedrich Nietzsche's analysis of Christianity and Western metaphysics, Lyotard suggests that the theatrical model of representation is indicative – indeed, one of the primary forms – of the widespread problem of nihilism (defined as the devaluation or nullification of life or experience through its subordination to or comparison with transcendent values, meanings or ideals). The theatrical form of representation, as we have seen, presupposes that meaning or its ground resides elsewhere, external to the experience – what is on the stage supposedly represents something absent (not directly present to the observer) whether it be in terms of a signification or referent. In short, in such a theatrical staging the meaning (or its guarantor) is transcendent to the representation (the theatre) itself.

This structural distinction between interior and exterior and the resulting deferral or evacuation of meaning to 'somewhere else', Lyotard claims, constitutes a form of religious or theological nihilism that has obvious political implications: God, truth, reality, an absolute foundation, a 'transcendental signified', an ultimate ground or an immaterial goal, all reside in a transcendent position that is appealed to in order to legitimise or authorise a claim but are not directly accessible in themselves. In this sense, meaning is structurally premised upon an absence or 'lack', of something unavailable yet promised or implicated – where things have no value or meaning in and of themselves except where they somehow relate to that which is not present. Plato's philosophy, which we have already briefly examined, is a clear example of this appeal to something transcendent as a type of legitimation for the authority of ideas as a truth and reality superior to the senses and the signs which signify them. Christianity, which historically is a hybrid of Platonism and Jewish messianic and Essenic themes, is yet another example – with God, heaven, grace and salvation, all partaking of this transcendent yet deferred position. Even psychoanalytic theory (whether Freudian or Lacanian), as we have seen, is not exempt from, but in many respects the fulfilment (the internalisation within the subject) of this nihilistic 'theatre'. Similarly, Marxist theory is a form of religious nihilism with its promises of eventual redemption (the bliss of a non-alienated, harmonious state and the arrival of a utopia (i.e. socialist paradise) free of the falsehoods and veils of ideology), and thus built upon the promise of something absent but yet to come. Seen from this perspective traditional Marxist and Freudian theories are still too mired in a metaphysics of truth, of promising a privileged access to an otherwise unavailable reality or ground.

Nor is it stretching things to suggest that capitalist forms of commodification and consumption thrive upon and are sustained through the perpetuation of this model – as people are driven to seek out commodities which seductively promise to somehow address the lack within them or put them in touch with transcendent elements that will provide reconciliation, or completeness, or plenitude, and yet which endlessly defer delivery on such promises. The 'here and now' of life is found inevitably wanting in respect to such an outlook.

The common strategy among all of the above forms of nihilistic set-up is to hollow out or evacuate an interior of meaning and to 'render' it external: to position it as transcendent (inasmuch as what is on stage simply refers to what is outside the space of representation). It constructs this division such that meaning is linked to a fundamental 'lack' or absence at the heart of representation: that is, its meaning or ground always resides elsewhere.[1] Lyotard calls this nihilistic absence or 'lack' generated by or implicated within the theatrical model by several different names but the most common is the 'Great Zero' (which can be God, truth, reality, the transcendental signified, etc.).

Lyotard claims that nihilism is a problem for contemporary politics, social analysis and even libidinal philosophy because theory as an explanatory model (and note the common etymological roots of the terms 'theory' and 'theatre') is deeply inscribed within this theatrical model – theory is structurally organised around the 'Great Zero', around appeals to truth or a ground, and therefore also implicitly nihilistic or theological. Theory, rather than being the answer, is itself part of the problem.

As an example Lyotard provides an extended analysis of semiotics and structuralism in light of these claims (although this analysis is applicable to any form of representation that appeals to something apart from itself as a means of explanation). In regard to semiotics he suggests that this happens in either one of two ways in relation to the sign. In the first, the sign in standing in place of something (a meaning), is itself devalued by comparison with what is signified – it is merely a vehicle or pretext for what is important, and can only function as such because it is not the thing signified. In the second, meaning is endlessly deferred through a network of differential signs (such as when one looks up the meaning of a word in a dictionary and is confronted by other words the meaning of which one must look up in an almost endless recursion). In the case of structuralism, this latter notion of a purely relational placement in the signifying network and the resulting deferral of meaning across the entire structure, reaches its zenith (or nadir), nihilistically colonising all domains of human endeavour.

Lyotard's attempt at addressing the problem of nihilism is developed at most length in *Libidinal Economy*, a dense and difficult text that presents a detailed elaboration of his mature version of libidinal philosophy. In this work, which Lyotard later denounced (perhaps with tongue in cheek) as his 'evil book, the book of evilness that everyone writing and thinking is tempted to do…A piece of shamelessness, immodesty and provocation,' he takes up a number of his earlier ideas which he substantially reconfigures. The style and claims of the book lost Lyotard many of his friends, who saw it (mistakenly) as a cynical or delirious apologia for the excesses of capitalism.

The book is quite remarkable in its chimeric form and begins with two intense images. The first image is a striking description of flensing the human form:

> Open the so-called body and spread out all its surfaces: not only the skin with each of its folds, wrinkles, scars, with its great velvety planes, and contiguous to that, the scalp and its mane of hair, the tender pubic fur, nipples, nails, hard transparent skin under the heel, the light frills of the eyelids, set with lashes – but open and spread, expose the labia majora…dilate the diaphragm of the anal sphincter… (LE 7)

The second image describes this blanket of flesh once splayed out as then subsequently stretched in to a strip and its ends twisted around and then joined to form a Möbius strip, a continuous and single-sided (topological) surface along which libidinal intensities travel in all directions. This band or 'bar' is then made to rotate so that it achieves greater or lesser degrees of speed and thus produces greater or lesser degrees of heat – such that when the bar finally slows down it appears to present alternating faces or sides. This is Lyotard's poetic way of accounting for how difference is transformed into the more constraining kind of opposition that usually characterises what Freud called the secondary processes.

Given his views on representation, nihilism and libidinal dispositifs, Lyotard faces here the fundamental problem of situating his own account of their workings in respect to these processes. How can he avoid falling into the trap of theatrical representation and nihilism (of presuming to know better, to have a privileged access to the truth) whilst inevitably acknowledging that his own theory is itself but a libidinal set-up? That is, how to account for his own contribution without positing a *meta*-theory, a transcendent and theatrical organising perspective?

His fanciful evocation above of the organism as libidinal conductor – which he happily concedes is not entirely coherent – is the first in a series of rhetorical 'moves' aimed at allowing him to advance claims whilst sidestepping the threat of nihilism. This image of the flensed skin as a spinning strip is, of course, a representation but it is a non-theatrical one: it depicts the body not as an enclosed space or volume separating an inside from an outside but instead as one continuous surface traversed by numerous intense passages of energy. It is no less a representational 'performance' or staging but it is one in which the performance is not separated from the meaning but coincides (perhaps paradoxically) with it in the same 'space'. This already sets up the stakes (and the purely rhetorical style) of what is to follow throughout the book, which reads as something that generates flows of energy rather than constitutes a space of meaning to be revealed or deciphered. Indeed, *Libidinal Economy* reads as if, through its provocative and transgressive mixing of genres, rhetorical styles, humour and seriousness, it were perhaps *Discourse, Figure*'s figural put directly to work and sustained across an entire text.

Lyotard's second strategy for dealing with the threat of nihilism is to abandon the traditional notion of critique that would otherwise underpin any appeal to truth – for critique implies that we have a superior (i.e. more truthful or more authoritative) position from which we can speak – denouncing this as just as complicit with nihilism and the theatrical model as notions of alienation, ideology, truth, etc. Moreover, he identifies such critique as a structure that already determines all the available positions within it: for 'the critic remains in the sphere of the criticized, he belongs to it, goes beyond one term of the position but does not alter the position of the terms' (DW 13). Critique, Lyotard suggests, is fundamentally reactive because it appropriates or prescribes meaningful responses to its assertions. To accede to its authority is to allow it to set the agenda and be captured or seduced by its promise of an 'answer':

> This trap consists quite simply in *responding to the demand of the vanquished theory*, and this demand is: put something in my place [i.e. change what is on the stage]. The important thing is this place, however, not the contents of the theory. (LE 104)

As an alternative to critique, and in an attempt at situating his own account, Lyotard proposes the notion of 'dissimulation', which stems from his theorising of the nature and workings of primary processes and libido. Primary processes are, as I described earlier, fundamentally positive for Lyotard, and he claims that by extension libido is primarily affirmative (inasmuch as what it does is simply a reflection of its own mobile and plastic nature) – it affirms its own productive power in its mobility. Contrastingly, negation or lack is, in an important sense, a congealing of libido into a channelling structure that plays a key role in the development of the secondary processes that characterise conscious thought. Basically, lack is libido turned against itself in the form of a fold or vacuole in which desire as force becomes converted into desire as wish. The upshot of this is that nihilism and negativity are not antithetical to libido (or even its absence) but in fact libido applied or invested in highly restrictive ways which thereafter generate a sense of 'lack' as a by-product – they are still instantiations of libido, but ones in which its affirmative character is deflected or more heavily regulated through forms that potentially reduce, compromise or curtail libido's very mobility and thus the intense range of its effects. In essence then, negativity as critique is a reactive articulation of desire; it turns back upon libido and dilutes, limits or retards the latter's capacity to act.

Confronted with this problem Lyotard's strategy is to 'dissimulate' his own position, or rather to dissolve his position within dissimulation. Taking his cue from Freud, who described his account of the death drive in *Beyond the Pleasure Principle* as purely 'speculative' (and also from Nietzsche's perspectivalism, evident in the latter's description of language as purely metaphorical in 'On Truth and Lie in the Extra-moral Sense' and his view of art as a useful fiction in 'Twilight of the Idols'), Lyotard describes his own efforts and representations in *Libidinal Economy* (such as the Möbius strip or spinning bar) as useful 'theoretical fictions' which do not disguise the fact that they *are* fictions. They are offered up not as truth-statements but as performatives, as images that directly evoke and provoke specific responses. Their value resides not in what they are but solely in what they enact: the types of effects they produce.

That Lyotard does not claim the status of truth for his views is central to his elaboration of a libidinal philosophy and has clear implications for theory in general. In this new approach Lyotard suggests that all the possible representations, viewpoints and approaches that one could potentially adopt (including his own) exist within a single continuum (of libido's distribution) differentiated not by whether they are more or less accurate or truthful, or right or wrong, but by the effects that they specifically produce – that is, not in respect to what they mean, but what they do. As such they are all forms of representation, given that any unmediated return to primary processes through representation is impossible by definition. One cannot evade or escape representation – it is simply a matter of which form or type of representation is to be invoked or deployed, and what further moves it enables or disables.

To seek to directly oppose or refute a position is to become caught up within the nihilistic pull of a representational 'black hole' from which one finds it increasingly difficult to extricate oneself. Instead Lyotard advocates pursuing the lateral possibilities that present themselves *within* existing structures, not in some program of reform that would assimilate such efforts but as strategic or tactical interventions that potentially destabilise or transform structures without a pre-given expectation of their outcomes.

This in turn leads to a modification of the way that Lyotard views the psychoanalytic dualism of the 'life' and 'death' drives – the fundamental forces which Freud characterised, respectively, as binding and organising energy in the organism and its psyche, and as destructively unbinding and dissolving those same connections both within the organism and between itself and its environment. In *Discourse, Figure* and the articles that followed in its wake, Lyotard – despite reconfiguring these 'drives' as neither strictly metaphysical nor organic but instead as different energetic regimes or modes characterising the way that libido operates – links the workings of the psyche to these drives. He tacitly accepts their opposed nature and, somewhat simplistically in retrospect, aligns the life drives with structures and secondary processes, and the death drive with the figural and primary processes (whilst suggesting that it is their entwined workings at the level of the unconscious which accounts for the fact that desire contains its own prohibition).

In *Libidinal Economy*, however, he presents a more complex picture in which he accepts that structures can never be fully avoided, as they are essential to providing modes of expression for desire, and correspondingly that libido is a pre-requisite for there being any structures in the first place. As a result, they always co-exist in varying degrees of mutual interdependence: thus both the life and death drives can be either constructive or destructive in their workings depending on any given situation. Libido (as energy) when it comes in contact with various investable elements (ideas, sensations, etc.) or potential blockages undergoes numerous processes of separation, diversion, filtration, channelling and damming from which structures arise and consolidate themselves. Conversely, the energy which fuels, sustains, and is captured and regulated by these structures nonetheless remains in excess of them and thus can potentially erode, dissolve or fragment them under propitious conditions. This means that sometimes structures can actually increase rather than decrease intensity – and as such, in respect to actual experience a structure is not automatically 'bad' in and of itself any more than libido-force is necessarily 'good'.

It is the very blurring of these various divisions that Lyotard refers to as 'dissimulation': that libido and intensities are both hidden within provisional structures (which otherwise present themselves as enduring or immutable), and channelled or released through those same structures. In light of the above, libidinal economy becomes an issue of pursuing in any given situation those elements within structures that will increase intensity and thus allow for difference, change and mutation.

Strictly speaking, however, negativity cannot be neutralised or cancelled through the application of more negativity, or through being critical – as this potentially augments rather than diminishes its power. Thus nihilism cannot simply be opposed or overcome by an act of will ('I deny that is the case' or 'I refuse to accept it'). The instrumental selfhood (the sense of mastery and self-determining subjectivity) that informs such actions only serves to further enmesh us within its constraints. Instead, drawing upon a lineage of the philosophical analysis of nihilism stretching from Nietzsche through to Heidegger, Lyotard proposes that we should explore alternatives to nihilism and nihilistic forms of representation through the promotion of difference, dissimulation, affirmation and 'passability', which in turn present new possibilities in respect to signification.

Dissimulation, in particular, provides a potential means of thinking, representing and acting that does not accede to the pervasive nihilism that devalues, negates or dis-intensifies life. Instead of futilely attempting to refute nihilism or destroy structures, we can strive to dilute or dissolve their respective tendency towards transcendence or stasis by multiplying or overlapping the number of competing perspectives that offer different effects: that is, we can employ 'open-ended', elusive or evasive strategies and pluralising tactics instead of direct confrontation. We can give ourselves over to intense experiences and the unforeseen events that they introduce within existing structures and forms of representation. The dominance of the theatrical model is thus weakened when we recognise that it is no more true (or any less false) than any other type of representation. It is what it does that matters and whether or not its effects enable or curtail further effects and explorations, for although all representations are fictions, their effects, for all intents and purposes, are nonetheless real – inasmuch as they determine our relation to the world around us.

These concerns apply equally to Lyotard's view of art during this period, in which he rejects offering definitive interpretations of works of art, if by 'interpretation' we mean identifying their significations in conceptual terms (i.e. this artwork says 'X', or it means 'Y'). His interest is solely in the operations they involve and the effects they produce:

> What is important in a text is not what it means, but what it does and what it incites to do. What it does: the charge of affect it contains and transmits. What it incites to do: the metamorphoses of this potential energy into things. (DW 9–10)

In a subsequent article, 'Beyond Representation', he elaborates on this view:

> An account of the economy of works of art that was cast in libidinal terms...would have as its central presupposition the affirmative character of works: they are not in place of anything; they do not *stand for* but stand; that is to say,

they function through their material and its organisation... and it conceals no content, no libidinal secret of the work, whose force lies entirely in its surface. There is only surface. (LR 158)

Here Lyotard seeks to evade the nihilistic demand that we decipher the 'truth' of the work, i.e. the meaning or concept supposedly either accessed through, or embedded within, a painting, a poem, a novel, film or performance. Instead in our responses to works of art he advocates what he calls a state or process of 'passability', a kind of 'free-floating' receptivity to artworks in which nothing is assumed or judged in advance, and instead where we open ourselves to the work's own dynamism, allowing ourselves to become 'good conductors' of its energetic flows.

Despite the shift in vocabulary from *Discourse, Figure*, where he speaks of the work in terms of its spatial arrangement in respect to the vicissitudes of desire, to this new way of speaking of libidinal surfaces traversed by energetic flows, Lyotard's view of art in respect to this issue remains relatively consistent from *Discourse, Figure* through to the end of his career: that art is about producing affects and we must open ourselves to them. Indeed, in *Libidinal Economy* he describes this 'receptive' conductivity in terms of what he calls 'tensors' (the word suggesting 'intensity' but perhaps also playing off the notion of tension and its discharge as depicted in Freud's account of the 'pleasure principle'). This involves a way of looking at signs quite different from the religiously nihilistic view proposed by semiotics and structuralism, because it acknowledges the energetic basis of all representation and allows for 'a dimension of force which escapes the logic of the signifier' (PW 64). In this regard the tensor is experienced as something traversing and ultimately eluding the subject, as something seemingly without meaning but not without effect.

Through dissimulation, passability and the tensor, and their respective capacities to multiply perspectives, libidinal philosophy seeks to differ from (rather than simply oppose) nihilism and to affirm differences. It is these intensities and differences that Lyotard believes are 'life-affirming' (not in the sense of Freud's self-preserving life drive but in terms of our existing in the 'here and now' as curious and passionate, mobile and sensuous, conductive and malleable transformers). However, these notions of dissimulation and intensification also present a problem that Lyotard becomes increasingly sensitive to throughout the latter half of the 1970s and thereafter attempts to address: that, like a throw of the dice, the results that these phenomena and activities produce are unforeseen and thus present no surety that their effects will (prove to) be life-affirming. Allowing oneself to be a good conductor of intensities still presumes some (minimal) degree of choice – inasmuch as one is faced with many possible means of conduction from one moment to the next, and such choice always requires a process of selection and evaluation. What to choose is dependent in part on how one chooses, and not all choices are equal. What then provides the basis for judgement, if notions of truth and falsity, right and wrong, are dissimulated into a concern solely with performative effects – particularly given that we can only know and assess such effects *after the fact*? Yet a further problem arises from this, for the pursuit of intensities will inevitably bring people into conflict, and in ways which are as likely to be nihilistic, cruel, violent, intolerant and unfair, as affirmative, generous, accommodating and just, depending on their perspectives and their circumstances. One person's affirmations, irrespective of their intentions, will sometimes lead to the negating or silencing of another's.

Once again this raises the thorny issue of evaluation and of respecting difference, and related issues of judgement, action, understanding and testimony. These are certainly not problems unique to libidinal philosophy, but nonetheless they remain issues that any philosophy of affirmation and action must address. However, although they are undeveloped and disturbing elements in Lyotard's libidinal philosophy, thereafter they become major concerns signalled primarily by his retreat from the notion of the libidinal (which increasingly he came to view as a metaphysical dead-end). This shift in orientation marked new interests whilst preserving certain thematic continuities with his earlier work. From this crisis emerged two distinct yet closely related thematic strands: on the one hand, an ethical concern with justice in relation to the differend (the respecting of the heterogeneity of differences between people and points of view) and, on the other, a concern with the heterogeneity of thought itself through the notions of the sublime and the postmodern.

Examination of the first of these strands lies beyond the province of the present study, but the second provides the subject matter for the next two chapters.

Chapter 3

The sublime

You have to find a way of saying it without saying it.

Duke Ellington

We thought we knew how to see; works of art teach us that we were blind.

Lyotard

Don't think, look.

Wittgenstein

In a series of works dating roughly from the early 1980s Lyotard introduces a new term into his philosophy, the 'sublime', which becomes a significant preoccupation throughout the remainder of his life. This concept still bears some relation to the role and attributes of the figural as a 'disruptive' element that challenges the familiar, but it is now additionally linked to the issue of what Lyotard calls the 'lack of reality in reality'. It is this complex notion that provides a new means of dealing with many of the issues, problems and concepts which he had explored in his libidinal philosophy.

Rather than presenting his views within a single work, Lyotard develops his account of the sublime and its relationship to art across a wide range of articles and studies. While certain fundamental elements or threads appear to remain consistent across all of these pieces Lyotard experiments with varying the emphasis from one to the next. The earliest references to the sublime appear in his writings on the paintings of Jacques Monory in 1981 and in the following year's 'Answering the Question: What is Postmodernism?' (which I will discuss in the next chapter), but it is with his subsequent articles on the work of Barnett Newman and the role of the avant-garde that Lyotard most clearly foregrounds the key characteristics of the sublime that will dominate his work thereafter. The most important and directly relevant of these works to his discussion of art, I believe, and the ones to which I will devote most, but not exclusive, attention here, are 'Newman: The Instant', 'The Sublime and the Avant-garde', and 'Representation, Presentation, Unpresentable' (all three of which are collected in *The Inhuman*).

As Lyotard's use of the sublime is complex and nuanced, but also highly selective, it is worth first retracing the origins and relevant history of the concept so as to better understand how he adapts it in respect to his own concerns. In its common usage today, the word sublime suggests a variety of different affective states such as awe, astonishment, profundity or shock. More significantly it often suggests responses that are seemingly contradictory – that an experience can be 'stupefying' yet at the same time 'thought-provoking', wondrously astonishing and yet terrifyingly awful. This strange, ill-defined and paradoxical aspect of the sublime is not a recent phenomenon but an ambiguity that permeates its entire history. In fact, the term 'sublime', which derives from Latin and is a translation of the Greek word *Hýpsous*, originally meant 'on high' or 'to raise aloft' (suggesting that one's gaze is in some way directed upwards). It was a term employed in ancient rhetoric (the oral art of persuasion, of leading others to one's point of view) to denote an elevated or lofty tone, or excellence or grandiloquence of speech, or otherwise heightened or intensified sensibility. Thus its use could evoke grandeur, nobility, awe, exaltation, provocation, even ecstasy or intoxication: in short, a sense of being profoundly 'moved' in some way. The first extended discussion of the term in this regard appeared in *Peri hýpsous* ('On the Sublime'), a fragmentary work written in the first century AD and usually attributed to Pseudo-Longinus (a figure whose identity has been much debated). Essentially this document is a commentary on the use of the sublime as a specific rhetorical device, a trope or figure of speech that alters literal meaning. It attributes to the sublime a wide range of associations whilst conceding the difficulty in precisely defining its nature or employment: in essence we recognise it primarily through its violent or forceful and compelling effects on listeners (which temporarily dispossesses them of their ability to reason), rather than any strict rules concerning its usage. Indeed, this general conception of the sublime as denoting incredibly intense emotion has been commonplace for a long time and in later centuries was often linked to an ineffable, ecstatic or numinous sense of the divine or mystical, or with the majesty of God or the Holy Spirit.

The translation of this work into French by Nicolas Boileau in 1674 and its subsequent circulation led to a renewed interest in and development of the notion of the sublime throughout Britain and continental Europe, particularly in relation to a number of ongoing debates concerning aesthetics (then a relatively new branch of philosophy). One section of the work in particular seemed to provoke much discussion, for although 'On the Sublime' largely details the discursive power of the sublime to move or affect others, in Chapter 35 it briefly links the sublime to the indefinite, the unexpected, the vast, powerful, ferocious or terrible, as these qualities appear in nature, citing examples of various natural objects such as storms, oceans, floods, waterfalls and erupting volcanoes (Kelly 1998: 32). This characterisation tapped into a growing appreciation amongst the aristocracy, artists and intellectuals for nature untrammelled by civilisation – forest rambles, fens, foggy moors and blasted heaths, and a vogue for Alpine treks where the ragged, asymmetry of crags and ravines, the frightening prospect of avalanches and landslides, and the immensity of mist-enshrouded mountain-tops, provoked a sense of awe and astonishment. This sense of nature's immense power was taken up thereafter by the Romantics and perhaps most famously evoked in Caspar David Friedrich's *Wanderer Above the Sea of Fog* (1818) (Figure 5).

These affecting vistas, however, did not sit easily with contemporary ways of describing and appreciating objects of intense interest, particularly a notion of beauty largely indebted to a plethora of sometimes incompatible notions and values inherited from the Renaissance, the Medieval era and Classical antiquity. This was a deficiency that the concept of the sublime seemed potentially able to address; however, it also led to the polarisation of the notions of beauty and the sublime (thus displacing other aesthetic terms). Within this newly developed contrast beauty was characterised in terms of symmetry, balance, proportion and harmony, and the sublime in terms of excess or disproportion, of that which strained at or deformed the very limits of comprehension, acceptability and taste. More significantly, the sublime came to be viewed as encompassing competing or potentially incompatible feelings – of the paradoxical mixing of, or rapid movement between, both pleasure and pain.

5. *Wanderer Above the Sea of Fog*, Caspar David Friedrich.

Two of the most significant contributors in theorising this contrast, and key influences on Lyotard's own perspective on the sublime, were the philosophers Edmund Burke and Immanuel Kant who moved the analysis and attribution of the sublime away from specific evocative objects towards the subject's own experience. If we look first at Burke's account in *A Philosophical Enquiry into the Origins of Our Ideas of the Sublime and Beautiful* written in 1757, we find that it is primarily an account that describes the beautiful and the sublime in terms of their respective psychological effects upon the viewer. Burke characterises the beautiful as domestic and agreeable in its orientation, as emphasising minor pleasures and trivial yet readily familiar or accessible sensations that accord with or are well adapted to the human sensory organs. In contrast, he aligns the sublime with intense encounters with whatever is strange, unpredictable, astonishing, obscure or potentially threatening, but most particularly with experiences wherein we are confronted with a sense of our own mortality. In essence, he describes the sublime as a response to those things which are felt as overwhelmingly terrible – whether encountered in actuality or the imagination – that link or mix together pleasure and pain, or fascination and repulsion. Thus Burke ascribes to the sublime an agitative intensity that makes the beautiful pale by comparison:

> [for] whatever is fitted in any sort to excite the ideas of pleasure and pain, and danger, that is to say, whatever is in any sort terrible, or is conversant about terrible objects, or operates in a manner analogous to terror, is a source of the sublime, that is, it is productive of the strongest emotions which the mind is capable of feeling. (Burke 1958: 39)

Moreover, he argues that the sublime is a feeling that not only causes terror but that fundamentally impairs or interferes with our capacity to think clearly:

> [N]o passion so effectually *robs the mind of all its powers of acting and reasoning* as fear. For fear, being an apprehension of pain or death, operates in a manner that resembles actual pain. Whatever is terrible, with regard to sight, is sublime too...(Emphasis added, Burke 1958: 58)

Burke's account emphasises several significant features in respect to the sublime. First, he claims that the sublime is a feeling evoked within the observer, as a result of being confronted by something threatening in its obscurity, indeterminacy or amorphousness – that is, in regard to something of which we cannot form a clear idea or perception. Secondly, in respect to nature he argues that the sublime is evoked when we are confronted by a sense of danger and correspondingly a sense of our own mortality, such as when we are in proximity to a raging inferno or a tornado or stand on the edge of an abyss. It is when we face nature at its most wild and powerful, and in a manner where we are rendered awe-struck or stupefied before forces that seemingly nothing could withstand, that we sense its power to annihilate us. This prospect of annihilation Burke describes as one of 'privation', the potential cessation of existence, of a sense of there being nothing more to follow – and we respond to this possibility with a kind of thrilling terror, a scenario wherein there is a suspension of normal life and an intensified sense of existence. The danger, however, is never such that we are directly confronted by imminent extinction, for if we were thus threatened we would be too intent on a desperate bid for survival to appreciate the experience. Instead the danger is safely viewed from afar, a place that brings us close to the danger such that we feel the possibility of a 'brush' with death but not so close that we feel our safety is ultimately compromised or placed at risk. This realisation that we remain safe in the face of such a threat subsequently generates what Burke calls 'delight', a sense of invigorating relief that we have been spared, that our fragile lives will continue. This delight, however, is not, strictly speaking, the same as what we usually refer to as pleasure. Burke dismisses the latter as the positive yet mild, comforting and conventional embrace of the familiar, but delight is a kind of 'negative pleasure' that springs solely from the removal of fear or pain. It is this movement between the pain of potential privation and the subsequent delight that marks our escape or release from it that constitutes the sublime encounter.

This type of encounter is not the only scenario wherein we might experience the sublime, however, merely its most extreme exemplar, for Burke claims that the feeling of terror and the sense of mortality that it introduces is potentially evident in any experience where privation looms. This is because it is closely linked to the way that such experiences impact on our very senses (and by extension our understanding): for when the clear outlines or limits of an object (or a clear idea of something) gradually give way to obscurity or indistinctness – such as in darkness or even its opposite, a blinding light – then a profound terror is felt as a result.

The above example explicitly links the sublime to the experience of a physical encounter, to the suggested threat of annihilation. However, Burke also links it to imaginative acts or artistic works in which a sense of something terrifying is evoked through an inability to clearly grasp what is meant or revealed: 'a privation of understanding'. Burke argues that this has significant implications for the appreciation of art where evocations of such obscurity through the withholding of clear meaning elicit anxiety or fear and a strong sense of the enigmatic or profound. It is striking that Burke links this sense of the sublime to literature (particularly poetry) rather than painting. His argument in favour of the former rests on his claim that the visual arts are fundamentally tied to mimesis (imitation). In order to indicate something recognisable they are compelled to directly replicate its physical appearance – its form and traits – and this places a constraint upon the imagination that receives such images. However, literature, because it relies on abstract symbols (that is, words) that do not resemble what they 'represent', is not subject to this same limitation and can produce stronger emotions through unfamiliarity or obscurity. In comparison, a painting of a particular scene or object when offered up to the eye cannot compete with the multiplicity of possible meanings and associations that the poet can evoke in the mind of a reader. Words conjure in the mind an ill-defined association, an unclear idea that is terrifying for the possibilities of privation it suggests or alludes to rather than for what it directly represents. Burke cites Milton's poetic description of Satan in *Paradise Lost* as an example:

> He above the rest
> In shape and gesture proudly eminent
> Stood like a tower; his form had not yet lost
> All her original brightness, nor appeared
> Less than archangel ruin'd, and th'excess
> Of glory obscured: as when the sun new ris'n
> Looks through the horizontal misty air
> Shorn of his beams; or from behind the moon
> In dim eclipse disastrous twilight sheds
> On half the nations; and with fear of change
> Perplexes monarchs.
> (Milton, cited in Burke 1958: 62).

He claims that this mixture of (sometimes seemingly unrelated) images gains its power from the incremental confusion, the indistinctness that they produce en masse and the subsequent relief we feel in our appreciation of them. It is in their very obscurity and indirectness that they make way for the feeling of the sublime.

Turning now to Kant we find that although he was greatly influenced by Burke and agrees that the beautiful and the sublime concern the subject and its affective states and not attributes of the object itself, his aim was not simply to account for the beautiful and the sublime in and of themselves but to fit these within a more comprehensive theory of cognition. His broader aim was to defend claims concerning objective knowledge from the attacks of sceptics and the more fanciful claims of metaphysics, in a manner that was not incompatible with the notion of moral freedom. This undertaking was outlined and developed across three successive works, the *Critique of Pure Reason*, the *Critique of Practical Reason*, and the *Critique of Judgement*, which sought to identify and evaluate the legitimate boundaries of our claims concerning knowledge, morality and judgement, respectively. A key part of this involved identifying those elements, operations or structures of cognition that do not derive from experience itself but are presupposed by it (a priori – hence, 'prior to') and therefore inherent elements or structural features of the sensory and cognitive apparatus.

The *Critique of Judgement* specifically examines these issues in respect to matters of aesthetics – that is, what claims can we legitimately make about matters of taste? Can such claims be universal and objective in a manner akin to scientific claims? What do such claims presuppose or require in respect to their form or content? In addressing these questions the *Critique* poses them in terms of judgement – that in making a claim we assert something. In his earlier *Critique of Pure Reason*, Kant restricted his examination to what he called determinate or 'determinative' judgements: that is, claims in which we assert the objectivity of what is experienced (something the appearance of which we can all agree is the case, such as a causal sequence), rather than merely subjective (something only true for you or me, such as liking the taste of strawberries). Essentially, determinate judgements organise particular instances or impressions in accordance with a universal rule.

Employing a cognitive model commonplace in his day, Kant describes this union ('synthesis' is his preferred term) in respect to related cognitive powers or faculties that we all share and which provide or organise the elements of experience. More specifically, the faculty of Sensibility provides intuitions derived from the perceptual organs, consisting of sensations of varying intensity, and arranged according to a priori forms of time and space (i.e. that everything we perceive is spatially and temporally ordered by the very structure of our cognition), to the faculty of Understanding, which then organises them according to concepts (or rules), and the products of which, in principle, provide the basis for objective knowledge. Moreover, the respective contributions of Sensibility and Understanding are united through the mediation of another faculty, Imagination, which is defined by its capacity to retain and combine intuitions over time.

In the final part of the *Critique of Pure Reason* Kant introduces a further faculty, Reason, into his discussion as a means of finally delineating the boundaries between the actual (what is) and the hypothetical (what might be). Sensibility and the Understanding working together can, in principle, provide objective knowledge but it is a patchwork affair with many loose threads and cul-de-sacs. Reason provides a special kind of concept, a sort of thematic horizon, upon which the efforts of determining objective knowledge can converge and potentially be systematised. These concepts that Kant calls 'Ideas' are speculative (concerning things which 'condition' or cause other things without being conditioned themselves): they hypothesise unities or totalities that reside outside the scope of experience and thus beyond verification by the senses, but remain useful in respect to their potential explanatory power. The examples of Ideas that Kant privileges in his discussion include God, the totality of the cosmos, and the human soul (although elsewhere he suggests that there are many others) – each of which can function as a hypothetical guide for our researches and means of ultimately uniting our investigations of the respective domains of nature, infinity and moral freedom. However, Kant insists that we must never mistake these speculations for objective knowledge, given that they have no corresponding object in empirical experience. It is in light of this qualification that Kant asserts that although we cannot know or demonstrate infinity as a part of our experience, we can meaningfully conceive of it.

In the *Critique of Judgement* Kant reconsiders the notion of judgement, allowing for the possibility that there are other legitimate kinds that do not conform to his original characterisation. Some of these types of judgements constitute a category that he calls 'reflective judgements' in contrast to 'determinate judgements'. The former type of judgement is characterised by the fact that it lacks any overarching or dominant concept in respect to the 'given' (we have no universal rule available under which a particular can be subsumed: instead such a rule must be sought for through an act of reflection). However, although indeterminate, it can still be said to be a judgement because of its form (that it asserts or makes a claim about something). According to Kant, although such 'non-conceptual' or 'indeterminate' judgements do not constitute knowledge (in lacking a rule for organising sensory impressions into a universal and objective form), they are experienced instead as internal, affective states – that is, as feelings of pleasure or displeasure (marked by intensive degrees of more or less).

The *Critique of Judgement* deals at length with two such types of reflective (non-determinative) judgements, aesthetic judgements (otherwise known as judgements of taste) and teleological judgements (which need not concern us here). In turn, Kant subdivides the first type of judgement on the basis of whether it concerns beauty or the sublime. In the case of beauty, an aesthetic judgement concerns a feeling of pleasure that the object (for example, a rose) induces in the observer, in respect to the perception of its form (that is, its spatial and temporal properties: contour, proportion, symmetry and so forth). These provide the spur for our contemplative appreciation and thus an aesthetic judgement.

Strictly speaking, such a judgement of beauty does not tell us anything about the object or its properties or qualities, but rather denotes the feelings that arise within us in response to these – it describes our encounter (in fact, the very act of judging), and not the object itself. This marks an important feature of such judgements for Kant: that they are essentially subjective. Indeed, because they are non-determinate judgements they cannot be objective in the manner outlined in the earlier *Critique of Pure Reason*, wherein Kant defines objective knowledge as characterised by its necessity and its universality (and by extension, its communicability). Nonetheless, Kant still wishes to show that aesthetic judgements (inasmuch as they are judgements relating to experiences that in some way can be mutually recognised, shared and meaningfully communicated) are in a sense universal and characterised by some kind of intrinsic feature that does not derive from experience itself. This notion that something can be both subjective (specific to me) and yet simultaneously universally valid (true for everyone) seems perhaps paradoxical and Kant presents a number of controversial justifications for his view.

His first such claim is that aesthetic judgements concerning beauty are disinterested and thus free (autonomous). He means by this that in respect to such judgements we can, and must, stand back from an object and appreciate it impartially or dispassionately. Thus we contemplate it without concern for its potential economic value, its utility or purpose, its moral applicability or its potential to gratify our own individual desires or sensuous appetites. We impersonally appreciate it in its own right as a singular instance and not as indicative of a kind or genre – that is, we are speaking of our feelings in respect to encountering this specific rose, rather than roses in general which would involve the application of a universal rule, and pleasure arises out of our awareness of our own capacity to view it in this way. In this regard, Kant suggests, beauty invites contemplation, reflection, harmony and a calming or restful repose. It is a kind of self-enjoyment of our powers for which the 'beautiful' object is largely a prompt.

Kant's second claim is that an aesthetic judgement of beauty involves a different interaction between the faculties than determinate judgement. The hierarchical relation of dominance that subordinated the efforts of the Imagination to the Understanding no longer pertains and a 'free harmony' between these two faculties comes into play, in which the former is free to associatively explore the object and what it evokes without recourse to any determining rules or principles of the Understanding. In this sense the Imagination also no longer plays a simply reproductive function (of presenting and combining the existing efforts of sensibility so that they can be subsumed under a general concept of the Understanding) but also a productive or creative one, in the associations and evocations it generates. As a result, there emerges a new accord or harmonious consensus between the faculties, reflecting the harmony that the viewer experiences in relation to the object itself, and which fills the recipient with an expansive feeling for life.

This leads into Kant's third claim: that an object which evokes a sense of beauty does so because it suggests a 'purposiveness without purpose'. Kant means by this seemingly enigmatic phrase that the object in its evocation of such free harmony seems well suited to our power of judgement, almost as if it was intended or created for this purpose (despite the absence of any evidence for this). A rose, when subject to an aesthetic judgement, has no purpose as such; it simply *is* – and yet its formal properties (its shape and arrangement) seem so orderly and coherent that it seems as if they were subject to some design the purpose or goal of which we can never know. In short, the object seems to intimate, yet fails to provide, a higher purpose or meaningfulness.

Kant's fourth claim concerns commonality. Although today most people think of matters of taste as simply subjective or personal opinions stemming from our own individual feelings or preferences, Kant's crucial claim is that despite their lack of objectivity (due to the absence of a determining rule), the a priori structure of pure judgements of taste concerning the beautiful still makes them universal in principle (if not in fact) and thus applicable beyond oneself (as a 'judging for everyone', as he refers to it). Kant means by this that our shared capacity for feeling and judging in much the same way (that our minds are similarly structured) allows us to call upon others to agree with us, irrespective of whether they actually do or not. The important point here is that it is the feeling, the aesthetic response, which is potentially shared as a result of our analogous sensory experience and that these aesthetic judgements in their shared, universal form provide the beginnings of a *sensus communis*, a 'common sense' (sometimes translated as 'public sense'), a shared appreciation which can, in principle, be communicated to others and thereafter provide the social (or as Lyotard suggests, 'normative') basis for a community of taste.

Turning now to the sublime we find that it is another matter entirely. It does not appear to accord with some of Kant's claims that characterise the aesthetic judgement of beauty – of something well suited to human perception and aesthetic appreciation which promotes soothing contemplation and a harmonious relationship between the faculties – and indeed its very excessiveness potentially unravels Kant's attempts to 'tame' and encompass it within the confines of his overall schema.

Like Burke before him, Kant characterises the sublime in terms of an intense and ambivalent response within the subject – felt as pleasure and pain – rather than as typifying a specific attribute of the object itself. However, unlike Burke, Kant claims that these feelings are produced within the observer when confronted not by obscurity or the prospect of annihilation, but by an intimation of the unlimited or the formless. He says that 'we call that sublime which is absolutely great' and adds 'it is what is great beyond all comparison' (Kant 1999: 64). However, he also distinguishes between two different modes of the sublime that he calls, respectively, the 'mathematical' and the 'dynamic'.

The first, the mathematical, relates to absolute greatness: it concerns physical scale and springs from encounters with objects or scenes that are colossal in magnitude (for example, mountains, the starry night sky, an abyss, waterfalls, the pyramids, etc.); the second, the dynamic, relates to absolute power: it concerns objects and scenes that generate a sense of immense, wild or overpowering force such as ferocious electrical storms, the raging ocean, volcanoes, earthquakes, tornadoes, etc. Each initially makes us feel painfully dwarfed by, or insignificant in relation to, a confrontation with something overwhelming. In the face of such encounters we cannot fully comprehend or encompass what is seen or what is being experienced. This is because the faculty of presentation (by which Kant now refers collectively to the combined workings of the Imagination and Sensibility) cannot adequately provide the faculty of Understanding with what it needs to conceptually organise and thus comprehend the experience: in short, no concept can be made available and thus Understanding is held in abeyance because Imagination, as the faculty of presentation and combination, has already failed to present what is required. Instead, an Idea of Reason (as a concept of the limitless or infinite) is evoked in the mind, but this only compounds the problem and initially intensifies the painfulness of the encounter, for there is nothing within the empirical experience that can correspond to it. What is seen evokes a sense of the infinite but the Imagination cannot match this perception to the Idea and instead it is felt as pain.

As such, both types of experience evoke a sense of the limitless and a dissolution of form that tears at the mind itself. Unlike the beautiful, which is calming, restful, relaxing, pleasing to the senses and harmonising to the mind and spirit, the sublime induces something painfully in excess of or at odds with what can be encompassed in perception. It introduces a discord into the collective functioning of the faculties, a fundamental and initially stupefying agitation that disturbs, or even violates, the self.

The earlier characterisation of the sublime as painful, however, is but the initial response of the observer to the encounter. The invocation of an Idea of Reason which introduces pain also provides the path to relief from it, provoking it to a higher level of thought, of conceiving something in the absence of a sensible correlate. In the case of the mathematical sublime, Reason makes us aware of our own immense cognitive capacity, testifying to our ability to mentally transcend nature and filling us with a pleasurable sense of our own power of reason – that we can think something that transcends what is experienced. In the case of the dynamic, the Idea which accompanies the act of feeling the power of the wild forces of nature whilst viewing them from a safe distance, also evokes within us a sense of our own potential moral strength – that even on those occasions when we might be physically threatened our sense of what is morally right (our freedom to choose to act in a way that is independent of such a threat, such as in an act of self-sacrifice) need not be compromised.

In each case, for Kant the sublime – after initially threatening the very integrity and unity of the subject – serves by way of Reason to ultimately affirm the self's primacy. As will become clear, although Lyotard agrees that the Idea of Reason may introduce a strange type of pleasure into the sublime encounter, he rejects any attempts at linking this either to the subject's affirmation of its own cognitive powers or its moral transcendence.

One final, important aspect of Kant's theory that we should note before examining Lyotard's own views is the former's claim that the power of the sublime, its capacity to affect us, arises out of what he calls its mode of 'negative presentation'. Kant means by this (drawing upon and modifying Burke's notion of obscurity) that it is the very unavailability of an empirical correlate for the Idea of Reason that intensifies the latter's hold over us: the less determinate the form or boundaries of an 'object' within experience (i.e. in respect to our perceiving it according to the a priori forms of time and space), the more powerful it potentially becomes as a result. However, this is only on the condition that in some manner we must remain aware of it, even if only indirectly through allusion or what Kant calls its 'abstraction'. Kant likens this negative presentation to the prohibition in ancient Jewish law against making images in the likeness of God. It is this very prohibition or privation that thus grants the 'invisible' or imperceptible deity an enigmatic power and profundity beyond the earthly – an excessive power of evocation that a more familiar or recognisable depiction would not be able to generate (such as we find, for example, in the portrayal of God as a benign and avuncular, white-bearded, old man so typical of children's storybooks).

Although this potted history of the sublime might have seemed an overly detailed digression, it provides us with almost all of the tools necessary to discern how Lyotard in his two articles on the American Abstract painter Barnett Newman adapts, modifies and challenges aspects of Burke's and Kant's respective accounts of the sublime as a kind of discord that mixes pleasure and pain. In these two essays, 'Newman: The Instant' and 'The Sublime and the Avant-garde', Lyotard overtly links Newman's artworks to an aesthetics of the sublime, particularly Burke's characterisation of the sublime in terms of privation and obscurity and Kant's notions of formlessness and negative presentation. As Lyotard notes, Newman himself was quite familiar with the notion of the sublime, having written his own eccentric commentaries on the subject, and sometimes choosing titles for his paintings (*Onement*, *The Name*, *Vir Heroicus Sublimis*) that foregrounded this association, so Lyotard's examination of Newman's work through this lens is not unwarranted.

In both 'Newman: The Instant' and 'The Sublime and the Avant-garde' Lyotard situates Newman's work in relation to the sublime initially through a discussion of time. In the first article he draws a distinction between the different temporalities or 'sites of time' attached to or embedded in any artwork: the time of its production, the time involved in viewing and understanding it, the time of its social or historical circulation, and so forth. However, the event – the time that 'the painting is' – is the temporality that most intrigues Lyotard and the one which, he emphasises, ultimately distinguishes Newman's *oeuvre* – not in respect to an obsession with the question of what time is or what it offers, which is not uncommon amongst writers and artists, but rather the unique response that Newman's work provides to the exploration of time: namely, 'that time is the picture itself'.

Contrasting Newman's large monochrome paintings (often traversed by one or two lines referred to as 'zips') with the work of Marcel Duchamp, Lyotard notes that two of the latter's most famous creations, *La mariée mise à nu par ses célibataires, même* (*The Bride Stripped Bare by her Bachelors, Even*, otherwise known as *The Large Glass*), and *Étant donnés: 1° la chute d'eau, 2° le gaz d'eclairage* (*Given: 1. The Waterfall, 2. The Illuminating Gas*), refer to or frame an event or encounter in terms of its anticipation or aftermath, and how the time they each invoke ultimately exceeds consciousness's attempts to contain or match it.

It is worth noting that Lyotard had a long-standing interest in these two works by Duchamp, having written a series of essays on them (collected in the book *Duchamp's TRANS/formers*) during his libidinal phase. Although these earlier essays primarily view the two works as dispositifs (set-ups) – as elaborately, complex devices that channel and circulate energy yet which ultimately are appealingly 'non-functional' – Lyotard also notes their temporal features: 'the time of the large glass is that of a stripping naked not yet done; the time of given is that of a stripping naked *already done*' (TRAN 36), where this stripping refers in each instance as much to the consciousness that is seeing as to the body which is seen. In respect to *The Large Glass* Lyotard emphasises the futility of seeking a definitive meaning: for the aim is 'not to try to understand and to show you've understood, but rather the opposite, to try not to understand and to show that you haven't understood' (TRAN 12).

In 'Newman: The Instant' these two works are briefly reintroduced in respect to how they promise and fail to deliver something, for each in its own way presents the mystery of time in terms of a revelation the potential yet ultimately frustrated consummation of which eludes our grasp. For example, in the case of *Given*, the viewer is confronted by a large wooden door. Should they look more closely they will find two small peepholes in the wood. Spying through these holes reveals a strange diorama, consisting of a background landscape and waterfall before which is positioned a recumbent woman, her face unseen, holding up a lamp. Most significantly, the woman is naked and the angle of the peephole directs the viewer's gaze onto a direct confrontation with the woman's hairless vulva. Here the door initially presents the viewer with a mystery; however, looking through the spy-holes for its solution reveals a yet greater enigma: sexual difference itself.

This work by Duchamp suggests through its two successive stages or steps – peering beyond the first set of 'holes' only then to find yet another 'hole' (a seeing with one's eyes that reveals a peculiar sort of unseeing 'eye' looking back) – a journey which ultimately leads nowhere determinate and yet which provokes our perplexed fascination. Newman, according to Lyotard, seems to go one better (whilst reducing the number of steps involved): whereas Duchamp's *Given* alludes to something beyond our reach, something as yet unpresentable, the paintings of Newman confront the issue both more and less directly, foregrounding the very moment of contact itself, of being 'touched' in some enigmatic way by the work as a sensible object. These paintings testify to the event's occurrence as it happens, in its happening, as the 'moment which has arrived' and yet as a moment devoid of determinate content, where 'There is almost nothing to "consume"' (INH 90). In this sense, Newman's works do not represent or depict an event, nor anticipate an elusive revelation yet to come – they are this event unfolding, inasmuch as they allow time 'to present itself' immediately to the observer. For this reason Lyotard refers to Newman's paintings as 'angels', for like their biblical namesakes they do not convey a message: their very appearance is the message (an annunciation); 'the messenger is the message' that both heralds and instantiates an occurrence (INH 79).

Lyotard claims that in such works by Newman as *Onement*, *The Name* and *Vir Heroicus Sublimis*, colour, line and rhythm each work to refuse any act of recognition concerning what is seen, instead forcing the eye into a direct confrontation or encounter with the moment of occurrence, the event, before it means anything definitive or can be assimilated into the narrative of everyday life. In these encounters the 'message is the presentation, but it presents nothing; it is, that is, presence' (INH 81). This 'presence' that Lyotard (drawing upon a line of thought in German and French philosophy that begins with Heidegger and passes through Levinas to Blanchot) sometimes calls the 'there is' ('*Il y a*' in French and '*Es Gibt*' in German), marks an allusive and elusive 'I know not what' ('*Je ne sais quoi!*') that confronts and 'touches' consciousness and in doing so challenges it with its own limits.

Each of these paintings announces, simply in being looked at, that there is 'something' important happening, unfolding in the moment, even if we do not know what it is or what it might mean (see Figure 6). Lyotard describes this occurrence, this event, as an ontological disturbance or dislocation of our sense of being, of a 'break' within consciousness and our sense of reality (a break which he also refers to in different works under a variety of other names: as a caesura, blockage, disruption, retardation, suspension, the 'blank' etc.) and a derailing of the subject's cognitive attempts at synthesising and reintegrating what it 'experiences' within any existing or recognisable frame of meaning.

In his follow-up article 'The Sublime and the Avant-garde', Lyotard expands upon this view of Newman's work as presenting an enigmatic confrontation with the occurrence, with the 'here and now' that he claims marks it as the 'object of a sublime experience'. This 'now' – this occurrence which is happening – is indeterminate and incompatible with the viewer's comprehension:

6. *Voice of Fire*, Barnett Newman (1967), acrylic on canvas.

> Newman's *now* which is no more than *now* is a
> stranger to consciousness and cannot be constituted
> by it. Rather, it is what dismantles consciousness, what
> deposes consciousness, it is what consciousness cannot
> formulate, and even what consciousness forgets in order
> to constitute itself. What we do not manage to formulate
> is that something happens ...Or rather, and more simply,
> that it happens...Just an occurrence. (INH 90)

Lyotard here similarly views this occurrence as presenting an
obstacle to its own assimilation within the subject's general
understanding and it is not difficult to see that he has little
sympathy with Kant's view that the sublime, after some initial
pain, ultimately affirms the subject's sense of his or herself at
a higher level. The value of the sublime experience for Lyotard
would seem to reside in its very capacity to defer, even prevent,
such a possibility.

Lyotard emphasises that this indeterminacy necessarily comes
before any issue of recognition or meaning. The question of whether
'something is occurring' (is it happening? *Arrive-t-il?*) is prior to
any possibility of addressing the matter of 'what is happening?':

> That it happens 'precedes', so to speak, the question per-
> taining to what happens. Or rather the question precedes
> itself, because 'that it happens' is the question relevant
> as event, and it 'then' pertains to the event that has
> just happened. The event happens as a question mark
> 'before' happening as a question. It happens is rather 'in
> the first place' is it happening, is this it, is it possible? Only
> 'then' is any mark determined by the questioning: is this or
> that happening, is it this or something else, is it possible that
> this or that? (INH 90)

Indeed, any attempt to grasp it directly as it is in this given
moment finds itself clutching at nothing recognisable. It breaks
with the continuity of time, which attempts to slot the 'now'
into the comprehensible and supposedly continuous stream of
experience, introducing instead a disjuncture, an asymmetry of

'before' and 'after' (for after this event nothing will be the same as it was before; everything is reshuffled in search of a thread). Not yet subject to an a priori form or synthesis of cognition (that is, a pre-given mental or perceptual structure), it introduces a caesura into thought, a disruption into the unity that supposedly defines and delimits the subject and its capacity for understanding. As Lyotard notes in *Lessons on the Analytic of the Sublime*: 'Sublime violence is like lightning. It short-circuits thinking with itself…The teleological machine explodes' (LES 54). Or as he puts it even more bluntly elsewhere: 'When the sublime is "there" (where?), the mind is not there. As long as the mind is there, there is no sublime. This is a feeling that is incompatible with time, as is death' (HJ 32).

It is worth pausing over this mysterious 'there', this 'presence' that Lyotard often refers to as a 'donation' and claims is ontological (as somehow related to 'being'). What is the context for his use of the term? Clearly, what Lyotard refers to here by 'presence' is unrelated to Derrida's famous critique of metaphysics, which was primarily directed at a philosophical tradition in which a self-affirming presence was assumed or sought as the foundation for knowledge and truth. In Lyotard's account this indeterminate 'presence' makes no claims to ground anything, for once grasped it is transformed (betrayed even) and thus made less than it is. Indeed, it works to undo such foundations.

If not Derrida then perhaps a better candidate would be the philosopher Martin Heidegger. In the case of the latter such a comparison is invited by Lyotard's own numerous references to Heidegger throughout his *oeuvre*. In fact, Lyotard devoted several books and essays to explicitly examining Heidegger's ideas or exploring their influence and implications in respect to specific issues such as the effects of recent communication technologies on art (and one could even argue that *The Postmodern Condition* was written, although not uncritically, with some of Heidegger's concerns as a conceptual backdrop). In his writings on the sublime in particular (indeed throughout the essays included in *The Inhuman*), Lyotard makes repeated references to 'being', the 'event' and '*Gestell*', three terms crucial to Heidegger's own outlook. To give but two examples, in relation to the first term Lyotard says in his discussion of Newman's work: 'An event, an occurrence – what Martin Heidegger called *ein Ereignis* – is infinitely simple' (INH 901). And of the second: 'It must certainly be granted that the donation proceeds from an X, which Heidegger calls Being' (INH 11). In these two remarks Lyotard acknowledges that art relates in some way to Being, likening this presence to a 'donation' that constitutes an event, and in doing so aligning himself with Heidegger's perspective. However, once we look more closely at what Heidegger means by these terms things no longer appear so straightforward.

To better understand their respective positions it is worth briefly looking at Heidegger's views on Being and art and their relation to his broader philosophy. In his early work Heidegger claims that Western civilisation is characterised by its amnesia concerning, and neglect of, a crucial question that resides at the original heart of philosophy: the question of Being and its meaning. Since the Pre-Socratics, this question (of what it means to exist) has been forgotten or repressed, and replaced by an increasing obsession with examining and determining the nature of particular 'beings' (e.g. *this* specific entity or type of entity, what it is made of, what traits it has) which has found its apotheosis in the materialism and nihilism of modern science – a process that has only served to further occlude and devalue 'Being'. Despite this historical development, Heidegger claims that human beings – which he refers to individually and collectively as *Dasein*, and later *Da-Sein* (literally Being-there or There-being, in both instances) as a means of avoiding prior humanist or objectifying associations – have a special relationship with Being: namely, *Dasein* is the only type of entity that is potentially aware of itself in this regard. It is the only entity capable of asking this question concerning its own Being, its own existence. Moreover, it is an entity able to redirect its way of life ethically, socially, politically, philosophically in respect to its awareness of these questions and a sense of its own temporality and thus its mortality: as such, it can potentially live a meaningful, authentic existence, informed by its own choices about how it wants to exist given the finiteness of its lifespan.

From the early 1930s onwards Heidegger reworks his ideas in the light of his reading of Nietzsche, particularly the latter's writings on nihilism. In such articles as 'On the Question of Technology' Heidegger begins to explore the consequences for modern society of this ongoing neglect of and withdrawal from Being. It is a view that expresses distress and bewilderment in the face of the alienation and inauthenticity of contemporary culture, of a soulless and desecrating modernity. It is also one deeply inflected with a powerful sense of melancholia, for what has (and is being) lost in modern life: namely, the organic bonds and the beliefs systems arising out of direct, relevant experience of the life-world that previously helped bind communities together. Fundamentally, Heidegger sees contemporary technology, and the scientific way of understanding existence, as embodying an even more remote relation to Being (and beings) than that which dominated in previous centuries. Heidegger claims that as a result modern society is increasingly determined by a calculative way of thinking and making sense of the world in which everything becomes a 'thing' (even other people), an object or material for consumption or exploitation and thus devalued or evacuated of meaning. This materialistic and quantitative way of conceiving and controlling the world and other human beings – which he calls *Gestell* (usually translated as 'enframing') – reduces everything it sees to a standing reserve or stock which must make itself available to be used up by humans.[1]

It is important to grasp that Heidegger is not criticising technology as such when he refers to *Gestell* but rather a way of thinking, a world view, a conceptual grasping that precedes and makes possible this perspective in which technology constitutes our principal form of contact with the environment and other people. It is a viewpoint or framing that shrinks the potential of existence, of the world, to little more than a series of calculative, efficient transactions, and forms of instrumental exploitation and masterful interventions – it is a perspective in which existence is nihilistically stripped of meaning. It constitutes a world, he argues, in which although the physical and communicational 'distances' between people may seem smaller and more easily surmountable than in the past, it is also an environment in which (in respect of being and community) they have never been so far removed from one another.

In his writings on art Heidegger attempts to address these issues and provide a different way of engaging with the world. In his famous article 'On the Origin of the Work of Art' (Heidegger's most influential statement on the matter), he outlines a perspective on art in the context of his view of Being. It is one that seeks to divest art of many of the usual assumptions it is burdened with (in the context of *Gestell*) whilst granting it a unique and privileged relation with human existence. Heidegger argues that a work of art is not defined by what it is made from, or its form, matter or 'message' (although obviously it is related to these in some way), nor the supposed intentions of whoever created it, nor any utility or commercial value attributed to it. It is still a thing (in the conventional sense of the word) but it is more than this. It is an object that can show simultaneously that it is an object and also the meaningful context in which it arises. It is, he claims, truth set to work in and through the work of art. Thus it illuminates and reveals (or 'unconceals' to use Heidegger's own terminology) the truth of *Dasein*'s relation to Being in respect to its 'life-world', or the world as it engages with it. This is not the objective and quantifiable truth of science – which assumes a measurable and verifiable correspondence between our experience and the material world – but a more profound kind of existential truth concerning the deeper significance of things in respect to how we live and value them. In this sense, the individual work of art in our encounter with it potentially marks what Heidegger calls an 'event' (*ein Ereignis* – sometimes translated as 'propriation' or 'enowning'). The latter is a tricky word in Heidegger's philosophy because it undergoes numerous shifts of meaning and accretes different associations over time. During this particular period, however, he mainly uses it in two different yet related senses: either as referring to making a 'clearing' in which Being and its meanings can come forth (as unconcealing or disclosure) and be *given* to us and engaged with, *or* as suggesting a happening that is not simply a temporal occurrence or historical fact (e.g. 'I went to work today') but something more profound, mysterious or inexplicable. In the latter case it connotes something that happens to *Dasein* (whether in respect to an individual or a society), which is unique to each individual or community, a 'lived' encounter which gives a new meaning to what is happening to them, making them ask questions and see things differently or afresh, and potentially transforming them (for better or worse) as a result.

Heidegger discusses three examples that make clear different aspects of what he means by an artwork's revealing of truth as an event. First he examines a picture of muddy work boots painted by Van Gogh. He suggests that this work illuminates the meaning of these objects in respect to the role or function they serve in someone's everyday life, a meaning that we would not otherwise notice. Such a work, he suggests, testifies to the lived relations from which it emerges, providing insight into the life-world of which it is a part.

Second, he discusses an ancient Greek temple. Such a structure is built upon and derives from what he calls the tension (or 'strife' as he refers to it) between the social and religious 'world' that it enables and concerns, and the potential or the possibilities inherent in the 'Earth' from which it is physically drawn: it is a dynamic relation between social meaning and the materiality of existence. But what is most important is that it both creates and provides a space (a world) in which a community's needs are met and its values shared. It is an environment where worship of the gods or spirits can take place, births and marriages can be celebrated, or deaths mourned. As such it creates and sustains the bonds that define and delimit a community: it brings a community together in respect to shared values, meanings and aspirations.

The third example he discusses is more vague yet also the most significant. From this period onwards Heidegger begins to view *Dasein* in terms of its relation with language (the latter viewed as a kind of house in which *Dasein* dwells) and as a kind of Shepherd tasked with caring for Being in all its manifestations. Language, with its ability to name things, plays a key role in creating meaning and this is most evident in what Heidegger calls its 'poetic' nature. This is a nature that all the arts partake of but which, for Heidegger, written or spoken poetry most powerfully evokes. He cites poetry, particularly the work of Friedrich Hölderlin, as being one of the few things (alongside which he also lists politics and religion) that is able to found a 'people' and thus an entire culture: to give it a sense of its own collective identity and situate itself in respect to the question of Being (of the meaning of existence and how one should live).

It is these aspects of the work of art in regard to its revealing of the truth of Being that Heidegger claims may yet enable us to see the world and our relationship with it differently and thus spare us from the devastating consequences of *Gestell*. However, it is also, he concedes, a receding hope, for such a barren and mechanistic world has less and less 'use' for such artworks with each passing day.

If we compare this view with Lyotard's own we see that in respect to Heidegger's notion of the event they are not necessarily incompatible inasmuch as they both conceive of it in terms of something both transformative and in excess of what occurs, but they fundamentally part company over the context within which it arises and the latter's way of linking it to art. For Lyotard the value of the work of art is its very resistance to providing a 'meaning' (and as will become evident shortly he adamantly refuses art the role of any kind of support or foundation for the communal bond). Presence in respect to the work of art is indeterminate. It is a 'donation' that is enigmatically unpresentable, both there and not there, eluding any attempt to grasp it. Indeed, Lyotard describes it as what 'will have preceded all touch, and will not have been of the world nor in the world' (HJ 34) and which devotes itself 'to marking on its body [both that of the work and of the viewer] the "presence" of that which has not left a mark' (HJ 33). In this sense, the donation paradoxically presents something (an event) by taking away something else (consciousness): it offers or gives, whilst simultaneously withholding; it advances, whilst withdrawing. In this sense it seems analogous to Heidegger's description of concealing and un-concealing; however, what it neither conceals nor reveals is meaning. Nor does it present us with a set of values and relations based in a specific life-world or a culture more broadly. If we return to Lyotard's earlier quote and follow where it leads, the difference finally becomes clear: 'An event, an occurrence – what Martin Heidegger called *ein Ereignis* – is infinitely simple, but this simplicity can only be approached through a state of privation. That which we call thought must be disarmed' (emphasis added; INH 90).

It is perhaps hardly surprising then that in 'The Sublime and the Avant-garde' Lyotard links this occurrence, this presence, the question of 'is it happening' in Newman's painting, explicitly to Burke's account of 'privation'. He argues that this blockage, the sublime encounter that we feel in the face of something indeterminate, is just such a state of privation, with its paradoxical mixing of terror and delight. In introducing a caesura in which the reassuringly familiar is refused, Newman's works disrupt the smooth flow of thought and thus deflect the grasp of an appropriating (even colonising) understanding, and in doing so raise the questions of *what* is happening, and of what has happened. However, these questions already presuppose and assume too much. Before knowing what is happening (or has happened) there is simply that it *is* happening: that something, an event, occurs before it is grasped by the understanding and forcefully slotted into the mosaic that constitutes conventional knowledge and experience.

Yet in doing so each occurrence will raise for the understanding that is in suspension the prospect of an ending, of whether anything else will or can happen, that there will be no more, nothing further to come, no more occurrences, no next moment, that the present will give way to the nothingness, to the annihilation, that is death. This prospect lurks as a shadow behind each successive instant of something happening – that at any moment it might, and will, stop – underlining the relief that ensues when yet one more 'moment' follows. The pleasure in this confrontation is not one that comes from a Kantian self-affirmation but instead a sense of relief in the 'privation of privation', that there is 'something' given, anything, even if we don't know what it is. Understanding, in a sense, is a continuous attempt (albeit futile) at forestalling the inevitable cessation of life itself.

According to Lyotard, it is a crucial feature of Newman's paintings, and the sublime feelings they evoke in respect to this privation, that they depict nothing recognisable or identifiable – instead when we look at one of these paintings we 'see' nothing more than large swathes of colour, sometimes bisected by a line that leads nowhere. In this sense they refute the conventional demand that a picture correspond with familiar elements of experience, that it show us the 'world' at some level, that it re-present a 'thing' or deliver a meaning or message. Strictly speaking, however, each painting is not a void – it is a strange no-thing but it is not a *nothing*. Each work gives us something (it presents an indeterminate) without this being some *thing* (this thing, that thing, any particular thing): but it is a 'presence' nonetheless. And yet, importantly, it is a presence, a moment, *felt* before being *known*, and, moreover, one felt as paradoxically both painful and pleasurable.

This refusal of positive 'content' and 'form' in Newman's works also links them directly to Burke's account of the sublime as an encounter with the obscure and indistinct. As noted earlier, Burke distinguishes between the arts of painting and literature as regards their respective powers of depiction and evocation, suggesting that the latter is the more powerful and therefore sublime of the two. Painting (and the visual arts in general), he claims, are inferior to poetry because the former, by its very nature, depends on figuration, imitation and thus recognition – it shows us how things appear in clear and familiar terms. It is obliged to render them visibly as they appear. However, in contrast, poetry draws upon symbols and mental associations that do not resemble what they evoke but instead rely on the power of imagination to conjure indistinct or ill-defined images in our minds that in turn generate powerful emotions. These evocations are less clear and more abstract, but all the more intense as a result for they exceed the limitations of the familiar and challenge the imagination.

Lyotard, however, unlike Burke, sees no real problem here. Painting is not in an inferior or disadvantaged position – it must meet the same needs as poetry but in its own way. Burke, after all, lived at a time and in a society defined by more rigid social and artistic values. He did not foresee the future existence of types of painting such as 'abstract expressionism' that pay no fealty to representing recognisable forms and objects. However, in our own historical era both painting and literature (indeed all the arts) have proven themselves equally capable of abandoning such demands for the recognisable or realistic in favour of the 'formless' and the perceptually and conceptually 'obscure'. As a result, Lyotard claims, all such modern works are potentially able to evoke the sublime as an intensification of ambiguous feeling through their refusal of figuration and imitation.

In Newman's case, and most of the other artists that Lyotard discusses throughout his later work, this usually involves a de-familiarising or de-forming of the image in a variety of ways, whether through subtracting, dissolving or multiplying elements within the overall image or an abstracting of the image itself. This commitment to denying the viewer a familiar, recognisable form and thus refusing to provide a distinct thought or feeling that can be easily communicated to others thereafter, also links the work to the 'formlessness' that Kant claimed characterises the sublime, as something which the faculty of presentation (sensibility and imagination) cannot properly formulate. But more importantly it directly pertains to Kant's account of the power of sublime evocation in terms of a mode of 'negative presentation': that of necessity the work can only allude to what cannot be presented directly, that which can potentially be conceived but of which no material example can be given, only felt. Yet felt in respect to a mysterious presence, for the sublime feeling 'bears witness to the fact that an "excess" has "touched" the mind, more than it is able to handle' (HJ 32).

Indeed, this power of 'negative presentation' as a means of approaching something unpresentable is what characterises and traverses the disparate endeavours of the avant-garde throughout the twentieth century. In the second half of 'The Sublime and the Avant-garde' and his later essay 'Representation, Presentation, Unpresentable' Lyotard provides a sketch of the historical emergence of these collective efforts, and one which clearly sets itself against the nostalgic, pre-modern hankerings that mar Heidegger's vision of art as a potential overcoming of *Gestell*. In these articles Lyotard acknowledges that the development and convergence of industry, techno-science and capitalism over the last century has forced the traditional arts into facing the prospect of their own increasing marginalisation, if not obsolescence. In fact, capitalist techno-science has created a world that 'needs photography, but has almost no need for painting, just as it needs journalism more than literature' (INH 119).

This is not simply because photography – and related visual technologies such as cinema – can more effectively satisfy the demands and conventions of representational 'realism', of the familiar conventions that are the common currency of social communication, but because more significantly, in doing so, photography has taken over and more ably accomplished the privileged role traditionally ascribed to painting since the Quattrocento: that is, of ordering the social and political world according to a monocular vision, and thus constructing an all-encompassing consensual reality. Through the use in painting of various perspectival and mimetic techniques, the social fabric from the Quattrocento until the early twentieth century has been identified, coded, collated and managed in accordance with the controlling view of a 'Prince'. This idea will not be new to those familiar with the work of Michel Foucault on 'epistemes', particularly his discussion of Velázquez's painting *Las Meninas* in *The Order of Things*. In the latter, Foucault argues that *Las Meninas*, which emblematically encapsulates the prevailing and determinate concerns of the era, is structured so as to align the viewer's gaze with the viewpoint of the Monarch whose presence in the scene, although suggested in a mirrored reflection depicted within the painting, nonetheless remains outside the painting as its controlling and masterful precondition. Similarly, Lyotard sees the history of painting as having ideologically managed our hierarchical conceptions of community and self-identity, of defining the 'programme of meta-political ordering of the visual and the social' through an analogous process of perspectival dominance.

Photography renders such a project simultaneously complete and redundant by both accomplishing and superseding it. In contrast to painting, whose practitioners were obliged to engage in lengthy, slow, costly and hugely detailed apprenticeships for the sake of acquiring specialised skills, the development today of ever cheaper and therefore more available cameras with automated 'one-click' functions that do not require expertise (such as automatic focusing, exposure time, lighting, transfer or materialisation of an image, and also nowadays mass media venues for image dissemination such as Flickr or Instagram) – of the 'industrial *ready-made*', as Lyotard describes it – has allowed everyone and anyone to participate in this huge defining project of organising space and culture. On the one hand, they engage (whether knowingly or otherwise) in its ethnographic documentation and, on the other, they complicitly subordinate all aspects of experience to it. The result of this anonymous assimilation is that ultimately it installs the controlling and ever expansive, commodifying gaze of capitalism everywhere.

Moreover, photography, in eclipsing painting, takes over the latter's more recent role of supplying an aesthetics of the beautiful, with its free, playful accord between the faculties. However, as an extension of industrial and post-industrial technologies, photography modifies this aesthetics so that rather than *seeking* a community of shared taste, it increasingly *defines* it in advance through the programmatic procedures and apparatuses that it involves and the common understandings that it prescribes. The general effect of this process is not just the loss of the 'aura' attached to the image (so famously described by Walter Benjamin), but also the destruction of the uniqueness of experience, and its replacement by pre-programmed, fabricated and carefully calculated thoughts and feelings, often indistinguishable from kitsch or cliché.

Thus challenged by photography and its related technologies, painting (and even a certain kind of photography at odds with this development) struggles to find a place and purpose for itself, and as a consequence moves into the domain of the avant-garde as a form of questioning or research which has no presuppositions and serves no broader social or political programs, whether therapeutic or integrative. Instead, painting must re-examine and re-situate itself and pose the question of 'What is painting?' (just as avant-garde photography asks 'What is photography?' and behind even these is the bigger question of 'What is, or can, be art?'), and sets out to seek and question the 'rules', the conditions for its own production. As Lyotard observes, 'painting thus becomes a philosophical activity' in which the 'rules of [the] formation of pictural images are not already stated and awaiting application' (INH 121). Instead it is confronted and driven by an interminable process of radical questioning:

> The doubt which gnaws at the avant-gardes did not stop with Cézanne's 'coloristic sensations' as though they were indubitable, and for that matter no more did it stop with the abstractions they heralded. The task of having to

> bear witness to the indeterminate carries away one after another, the barriers set up by the writings of theorists and by the manifestos of the painters themselves. (INH 103)

The avant-garde, in a patchwork series of advances and retreats – and through approaches and procedures that are often more subtractive than additive in nature – questions and contests the technical and conceptual presuppositions previously attached to its fields of practice.

In the case of painting, over the last century this has involved an investigative questioning that goes beyond simply challenging what constitutes appropriate subject matter, towards deconstructing the use and application, both singly and in combination, of every aspect of the medium and practice, including: linear perspective, colour values, tonality, pigment, texture, brushes, the support (e.g. canvas and stretchers), the frame, the size of the image, the place of exhibition or venue, the existence of a discrete physical object, and so forth. Clearly, this is not some naively prescriptive pursuit of the sort demanded by Clement Greenberg: namely, that a medium finds its essence in a definitive, formal feature (which in the case of painting he claimed was its 'flatness') (INH 103).

In both seeking to present images or textures or experiences that cannot be presented by conventional photography and cinema, and addressing the general issue of offering something that cannot be presented according to the prevailing or established rules and procedures concerning representation, painting and the avant-garde visual arts in general confront the issue of visibility itself (just as avant-garde music confronts the issue of what constitutes the sonic or audible and thus challenges tonality and harmony, and literature confronts the limits and foundations of narrative and the discursive – each looking for what somehow enables it, without itself being grasped or directly presentable). In this way painting begins 'to overturn the supposed "givens" of the visible so as to make visible the fact that the visual field hides and requires invisibilities' (INH 125) and in doing so makes 'seen what makes one see, and not what is visible' (INH 102). Indeed, the avant-garde commits itself to the 'abstraction' of Kant's negative presentation: that is, not to presenting the unpresentable – which would be impossible – but presenting the fact that the unpresentable *is* unpresentable, to 'negatively presenting the unpresentable', both alluding to and bearing witness to the impossibility of presenting this presence that is always presupposed in what is given: 'What art can do is bear witness not to the sublime, but to this aporia of art and to its pain. It does not say the unsayable, but says that it cannot say it' (HJ 47).

Painting, in foregrounding this problem, abandons to conventional photography and film and the fabricated and programmed images of contemporary cultural production the supposed vicissitudes of the beautiful, instead turning itself towards the aesthetics of a sublimity unregulated by 'common sense', or delimited by a community of shared taste. In its place it produces singular 'monsters' which, on the one hand, affront and perplex the public, challenging and destabilising its expectations and sense of the 'real', its identity and its power of judgement, and its dependence on commodities that can quickly and easily be consumed, and which, on the other, resist the programmatic dictates of the marketplace and the prescriptive political and social agendas of the state's cultural commissars and the 'public intellectuals' of the mass media.

In claiming that an aesthetic judgement of taste concerning beauty is a non-conceptual or reflective judgement defined solely by a feeling, and furthermore a 'sentimentality' which in principle is universal (i.e. that can be shared and communicated and thus form the basis of a communion and community), Kant describes a form of communication that does not involve such determinate concepts of understanding. On the basis of such a judgement Kant posits a community of shared and stabilised taste (a *sensus communis*), but what Lyotard wonders (in such essays as 'The Sublime and the Avant-garde' and 'Something Like: Communication...Without

Communication') would we find if instead we examined the notion of communication in respect to a sublime feeling. Then perhaps the notion of a community of taste could not be presupposed, for the sublime encounter, the 'is it happening', provides no such common ground, even in respect to a feeling. Indeed, unlike the feeling of beauty, which encourages calm, contemplative and harmonious repose linked to an appreciation of form, instead the 'formless' or deforming sublime engenders an ontological assault and agitation in which the subject itself is placed into question, and its attempts at mastering time are nullified. Here we find a 'communication' without concept or subject (at least in any recognisable manner), which does not presuppose either an objective determinate judgement nor a harmonising, non-determinate judgement of taste, and which is not addressed to anyone (for it has no message, no identifiable content) – so in what sense can it still be said to be communication? In the case of the sublime, as distinct from beauty, it is, perhaps ironically, not a community based simply on something analogously felt among a shared number but a presence that introduces a caesura within the subject's sense of linear time and thus a shared loss (of selfhood). It is a 'community' only in the sense that the artwork's recipients' existing social and ideological fabric is torn asunder – it is a 'negative' (comm)union, characterised not by an accord of appreciation but by a shared feeling of dispossession and annulment that Lyotard describes as a 'passability to lack', as a receptivity to what may come that can no longer assume that the social 'real' is able to consistently provide appropriate and communicable forms in respect to time and space. It is within this context that the avant-garde commits itself to relentlessly dismantling those overarching perspectives that have organised experience throughout the twentieth century, and it is to a broader examination of these issues that we now turn.

Chapter 4

The postmodern

> All endings are happy endings, just by being endings, for even if a film finishes with a murder, this too can serve as a final resolution of dissonance.
>
> Lyotard

> The suffering of thinking is a suffering of time, of what happens.
>
> Lyotard

> I can't go on, you must go on, I'll go on, you must say words, as long as there are any...
>
> Samuel Beckett

As several commentators have noted, Lyotard's work from the late 1970s onwards marks a shift from a preoccupation with space to an increasing concern with time and temporality, filtered through the examination of, first, narrative and then the postmodern and the sublime. This re-orientation also marks a parallel turn away from the terminology of the libidinal (although not necessarily away from Freud) towards a more Kantian vocabulary.

The notion of the postmodern, in particular, offers Lyotard a new way of presenting and reflecting upon old themes and issues related to the arts. In this chapter, I will examine three exemplary works – *The Postmodern Condition*, 'Answering the Question: What is Postmodernism?', and 'Rewriting Modernity' – each of which offers a distinct yet inter-related set of insights concerning Lyotard's view of the postmodern. The first examines his outline of the notion of the postmodern, the second clarifies his position and links it to other concerns such as the sublime and the arts more generally, and the third presents the broader perspective within which Lyotard situates the postmodern. My aim in examining these works is to demonstrate that Lyotard's ideas about the postmodern are not indicative of a period or theories that are passing out of fashion (or already obsolete), but are still, in fact, crucially relevant to culture and the contemporary arts – perhaps more so than ever.

The initial context for Lyotard's exploration of the notion of the postmodern was his developing interest in the latter half of the 1970s in the role and significance of 'narrative' as a structure of meaning and communication, as a form of social organisation, and more significantly, as a site of potential resistance to the social and political status quo. This interest focused on how all cultures rely on 'storytelling' as a privileged form for ordering experience into meaningful arrangements or sequences communicable by language, and thus providing a means of making sense of themselves, and of understanding and shaping their collective past and ongoing existence. In particular, Lyotard examined 'smaller' narratives that resisted assimilation into the dominant views or controlling institutions of Western society, counter-narratives that he referred to as 'pagan' so as to mark their impiety, irreverence, indigestibility and potential challenge to authority and social conformity. More specifically he was interested in how, in the absence of fixed criteria, we choose between the competing claims implicit in such a multiplicity of stories, whilst still according some kind of justice to them.

It was hardly surprising then that on being commissioned by the Council of Universities of the Provincial Government of Quebec to prepare a synoptic report on the state or condition of knowledge in contemporary 'developed' societies, that Lyotard would do so in terms of narrative. What was perhaps surprising at the time was his linking of this approach to the word 'postmodern', a term to which he had been introduced by the literary critic Ihab Hassan, at a conference in America in the mid-1970s. Lyotard readily admits in several places that the term came loaded with a number of prior meanings and cultural associations (indeed a history stretching back at least a hundred years and which had already been in circulation in artistic and literary circles for at least two decades). However, it was his intention to deploy the term as a means of strategically and provisionally intervening in contemporary debates concerning what was occurring socially, culturally and politically in Europe and America. It was a decision that in many ways Lyotard came to regret, given the way the term subsequently became his enduring 'legacy' – so attached to his name that it was often treated as kind of a shorthand for his philosophy as a whole, and yet which constituted a legacy that bore little relation to his actual ideas and arguments.

The Postmodern Condition was published in French in 1979 (and translated into English five years later). Despite its brevity it is the most well known of all of Lyotard's works. He did not personally regard the book as particularly important (viewing it more as a general preliminary sketch of the direction his thought was taking at the time than a rigorously argued work) – and he certainly did not anticipate how widespread would be its influence. As a result, Lyotard spent a number of years addressing through numerous articles and lectures what he perceived to be the numerous recalcitrant misrepresentations and misunderstandings of his claims (particularly their misapplication in the fields of literary studies, media studies and cultural analysis) that arose in the book's wake. But part of *The Postmodern Condition*'s significance, and its success, was that it gave the word 'postmodern' a currency and degree of publicity (misrepresentations aside) that it had previously lacked, moving it into the foreground of scholarly and cultural debate.

Before detailing Lyotard's account of the postmodern it is worth noting a few factors that potentially confuse matters, as well as briefly examining some of the loosely related, yet competing understandings, of the term that have unfortunately come to eclipse it in the intervening decades. First, the title of the work itself already presents difficulties. It consists of two key terms. The first, the 'postmodern', itself already contains another pre-existing term, the 'modern'. The latter is usually viewed as referring to either 'modernity' (viewed as the succession of social, political and economic transformations that have characterised the West since the fifteenth century and which accelerated and intensified with the advent of the European Enlightenment in the eighteenth century and then industrialisation), or 'modernism' (the aesthetic umbrella term used to describe a variety of artistic or cultural responses to the effects of modernity). In turn the word 'post' here as it is conventionally understood can mean something which follows 'after' (chronological succession) and thus continues the modern (in either sense above) or 'anti-' in the sense of reacting against it (i.e. in opposition to). The conjoined term 'postmodern' is often then understood in academic circles (and somewhat confusingly for the layperson) as referring to a transformation of, or response to, either modernism or modernity (where the latter entails the former), and can refer to this response in either positive or negative terms (whether wholesale or selectively in part) as an intensification *or* refutation of one or the other. If we now look at the word 'condition', the usually neglected half of the coupling, in its more general usage it can also mean either one of two things: it can refer to an existing state of affairs (as the book's subtitle seems to suggest) or to that which influences or makes something possible, as when we say 'Y is conditional on X'. As we will see Lyotard's own use of these terms is even less straightforward than these definitions would suggest as he claims that the postmodern is not simply reducible to a matter of chronology or the effects associated with its appearance, and indeed his views are not meant to simplify these matters but rather to make our grasp of them more complex.

The next point worth considering also relates to the term in respect of its more common appearance, where it carries a suffix: postmodern*ism*. We should be aware that most critics or theorists do not speak of the postmodern as such but rather of postmodern*ism* and it is important to note that Lyotard rarely uses this term in his own writings and on those few occasions when he does, he is usually citing the ideas of others associated with it. Instead he almost always refers to the 'postmodern' for reasons that will become clear. Similarly, he rarely uses the word 'modernism', preferring the term 'modern' instead.

A few comments are also necessary concerning these other perspectives usually referred to under the banner of postmodern*ism* before turning to Lyotard's own views. Apart from the populist notion of postmodernism prevalent in the mass media (where it serves as a catch-all for the weird or nonsensical, endless in-jokes, or the peculiar claim that 'everything is relative') an incredible diversity of versions have been offered up by theorists, critics and cultural commentators, struggling for recognition in the marketplace of ideas. Among the more well-known contributors we might include Charles Jenks, Robert Venturi, Kenneth Frampton, William Spanos, Fredric Jameson, Hal Foster, Linda Hutcheon, Charles Altieri, Andreas Huyssen, Richard Rorty, Brian McHale, Perry Anderson, Jean Baudrillard, Alex Callinicos and Zygmunt Bauman. After 30 years, in truth, their number is legion. Even Pope John Paul II weighed in to the debate in the late 1990s with an encyclical on postmodernism.

Although each of these figures offers up and promotes a particular version of postmodernism, two identifiable features tend to characterise, even define, almost all of their respective views. The first is the presentation of a kind of 'checklist' of identifiable and exemplary postmodern characteristics or traits linking it to one or more artistic media or cultural forms, usually in terms of stylistic techniques and devices but also occasionally conceptual features, including but not restricted to: *mise en abyme*, self-reflexivity, meta-fiction, eclecticism, the cultural 'dominant', neo-ornamentation, generic hybridity, recycling, multi-media practice, the de-centring of the subject, the promotion of style over substance, the erosion of the boundary between high and low culture, pastiche, the loss of historicity, and simulation. As a result, the postmodern came increasingly to be associated in academic circles with the 'death' of the modernist notions of artistic originality, authenticity and the uniqueness of the art object, on the one hand, and a sense of creative and cultural exhaustion (even as an index of the declining fortunes of Western political power signalling the rise and triumph of nihilism), on the other – a feeling also linked to the fatigue induced by the endless arguments and internecine squabbles that marked public debate, as artistic reputations and academic careers were made and unmade.

The second feature, which I have already touched on, involves viewing postmodernism as explicitly denoting a *periodisation* – a movement from one period or era or stage to another (i.e. as chronologically or causally following modernism or modernity as either continuation or repudiation). Indeed, this was one of the most persistent and vexing problems that beset the reception of *The Postmodern Condition*: the mistaken assumption by its critics that Lyotard was primarily employing the concept of the postmodern in a periodising sense. This was a misunderstanding that he spent much time and energy refuting in a number of subsequent articles (in fact, half of the essays included in *The Postmodern Explained to Children* are concerned with clarifying his position and rebutting a number of misconceptions and criticisms). The word 'postmodern', docked of its tail, was Lyotard's obvious attempt to evade the associations of periodisation and evolution that usually accompany the use of the suffix 'ism' in theoretical debates. Unfortunately, most of his critics did not appear to notice.

It should be acknowledged, however, that this mistaken impression was perhaps initially fostered in part (if unintentionally) by Lyotard himself, due to the wording of his claims in the introduction and the first few pages of the *The Postmodern Condition* (keeping in mind that Lyotard never anticipated that this work would go on to receive such wide-spread attention). There he states that the 'object of this study is the condition of knowledge in the most highly developed societies. I have decided to use the word *postmodern* to describe that condition' (PC xxiii). A little further on he adds: 'I will use the term modern to designate any science that legitimates itself with reference to a metadiscourse...making an explicit appeal to some grand narrative...Simplifying to the extreme, I define postmodern as incredulity towards metanarratives' (PC xxxiii–xxxiv). And on the very first page of the main body of the text he begins: 'Our working hypothesis is that the status of knowledge is altered as societies enter what is known as the postindustrial age and cultures enter *what is known as the postmodern age*' (emphasis added; PC 3).

These three interrelated claims certainly create the impression that Lyotard is speaking of the postmodern here as somehow linked to, or implicated within, a recent socio-economic transition occurring in Western nations. Reading the remainder of the book, however, slowly reveals (and this was meant to be reinforced by the inclusion of an article originally written in 1982 as an appendix in the English edition) that he is not saying, however, that this is necessarily what defines, inaugurates or circumscribes the postmodern as such. Obviously the postmodern is related to this historical transformation but it is not reducible to it. Or put slightly differently, the scepticism towards meta-narratives or authoritative claims which character-ises the postmodern is not unique to contemporary or 'post-industrial' society – these merely mark a historical juncture where its influence or 'presence' can be seen to be widespread, and perhaps even comes into its own. This is not simply a matter of interpretative 'hair-splitting', because Lyotard is trying to make an important point that is otherwise obscured – a point that he returns to repeatedly in subsequent work: that the modern and the postmodern are closely related modalities, rather than historical periods, and thus both the post-industrial 'era' and what precedes it are striated by both modern and postmodern ways of thinking and being.

If we now turn to the actual text we find that *The Postmodern Condition* begins with some general comments about knowledge which, given that the book was written over thirty years ago, have since proven remarkably prescient, although at the time they probably seemed more like science fiction. Essentially, Lyotard claims that knowledge in 'computerised societies' is increasingly identifiable as a commodity, as something to be bought and sold, which is disengaged from or indifferent to fundamental social or human needs. Part of what he is suggesting, although he does not state it quite so bluntly here as in later articles, is that knowledge is viewed in terms of its capacity to be transformed into and exchanged as 'information', a supposedly neutral form of data (the computer 'bit') which can be transferred across numerous communicational platforms (and which by extension functions increasingly as the new 'currency' of capitalism). In practical terms this is facilitated by developments in computerisation and telecommunications that are 'changing the way in which learning is acquired, classified, made available and exploited' (PC 4). This is also evident in the increased focus on models of rapid coding and decoding indebted to the study of language, communication, cybernetics and telematics (PC 3–4).

Moreover, knowledge in contemporary society, according to Lyotard, is not just one commodity amongst many, but perhaps the pre-eminent resource (rapidly eclipsing oil and gold) that nation states compete for and the distribution of which they seek to control. Unfortunately, however, the economies of most modern nation states can no longer accommodate the degree of investment required for the research and exploration that otherwise sustains such a knowledge-driven economy, and so they are relinquishing their sovereignty to multi-national corporations that do have this capacity, but which also have no ethical obligation to national constituencies (and often even their shareholders), let alone humanity in general. It is a global scenario in which the ethics of research take second place to the pursuit of profit (for example, the human genome project which has enabled private corporations to patent information concerning data on specific genes related to a variety of treatable illnesses).

This raises a number of questions: What kind of knowledge is regarded as legitimate? How are different types of knowledge valued? How and why has this situation come about? Lyotard's combined answer is that the changing status, form, value and role of knowledge is tied not to technology itself, which is merely a symptom of what is occurring rather than its cause, but to changes in the way that the West views itself and its place in the world at large: in short, the kinds of stories that the West collectively tells about, and to, itself so as to make sense of and thus justify the what, why and how, of its ongoing existence.

This is where Lyotard re-introduces and reworks his earlier 'pagan' theories about narrative and its social role. He argues that all societies 'ground' themselves in stories about who and why they are, where they are from, and who is included or excluded from them. In traditional societies these stories, basically mythic and oral in form and presentation (although some of these same notions apply to early literate cultures), consisted of structures in which addressor and addressee knew their place – indeed, the story defined and authorised their respective (and usually fixed) positions within the storytelling structure *and* the story recounted.

The telling of such stories provided, reproduced and reinforced prevalent views of how such a society came about, justifying and thus preserving the status quo through an understanding of the present in relation to some persistent notion of the past. This is why oral societies are often resistant to significant change, except where such change arises contingently. Essentially, they view themselves through narratives that serve to legitimise their traditional social structure (and its accompanying world view) through appeals to the past – whether real or imagined. However, these stories over time were absorbed within, and reorganised, and sometimes even silenced, by what Lyotard calls 'meta-narratives'. Although usually larger in form, it is not their size or scale that defines them. They are not simply 'bigger stories' – a point often lost on both Lyotard's advocates and critics – but a very different type of structure. Meta-narratives do not simply reproduce the same (usually cyclical or self-affirming) way of looking at things, but instead orient everything that they assimilate towards a particular *telos* or goal that motivates and justifies their efforts and existence. In other words, they view and organise the present in relation to an envisaged future or end point.[1] Indeed, in a sense, these structures are akin to what Lyotard was describing half a decade earlier as nihilistically 'transcendent' or theatrical dispositifs.

There have been numerous such meta-narratives operating throughout history and sometimes these undergo diverse transformations or even combine or operate in alliance. In fact, several such meta-narratives still compete for attention in contemporary society, although unlike in the past no single meta-narrative exclusively dominates. The most enduring and influential such meta-narrative in the history of the West has been Christianity, which has undergone numerous modifications and produced a variety of sometimes almost unrecognisable offshoots. More specifically it has colonised the smaller narratives of Europe (the transformation of pagan festivities into Christmas being an obvious example). However, what is most significant about Christianity and characterises its enduring influence is its promise of redemption or salvation in the form of a paradise yet to come, if we but obey its requisite demands or dictates and direct all our efforts to bringing about this state of affairs. This structure (and its promise of an achievable utopia) has survived and informed in a displaced manner almost all of the subsequent meta-narratives that have shaped the West – that is to say, the specifics of their respective language and dictates appear different but their structure and goals remain analogous.

Lyotard argues that the advent of what today most historians and sociologists would call 'modernity', signalled by the transition from feudalism to capitalism, the Renaissance and the humanistic notion of the 'individual', and the beginnings of empirical science (in the form that we would now recognise it), marked a fundamental mutation in the form and status of the Christian meta-narrative, that congruently began to reshape the way that the West viewed itself. But it is the eighteenth century European Enlightenment, in particular, that marks the emergence from this scenario of a new utopian meta-narrative, characterised by two distinct yet closely related strands or forms related to the French *philosophes* on the one hand, and German Idealism on the other. These meta-narratives – which with deliberate irony Lyotard also calls 'grand' narratives – organise Western society either in terms of a narrative of speculation (the pursuit of absolute knowledge) or of emancipation (working to make mankind free of exploitation, ignorance and superstition), or some fusion of the two. Both strands embrace a notion of 'progress', of a movement towards the betterment and fulfilment of mankind (as masterful and self-realising agency or spirit), and thus the pinnacle and measure of all things. Historically, these meta-narratives in turn spawned further mutations, such as Marxism and Liberalism, in which these speculative and emancipatory aims were recast in different terms – economic determinism and individual autonomy (non-alienated labour and self-fulfilment), respectively.

However, the twentieth century has brought us face to face with the obvious failings of these meta-narratives, their inability to deliver on their universalist and utopian promises: the Stalinisation of the Russian Revolution, totalitarianism in Nazi Germany and Fascist Italy and Spain, the economic depression of the 1930s, two world wars and the subsequent Cold War all generated an increasingly sceptical response towards the universalism (the homogenising 'one size fits all' ethos) that underlies them. In subsequent articles included in *The Postmodern Explained to Children* Lyotard fleshes out this list to include a number of other contributing factors such as the Holocaust, pollution and environmental degradation and the threat of nuclear annihilation, but to these we can we can add even further failings: eugenics, chemical and viral warfare, ethnic cleansing, the expansion of unwieldy and often self-serving bureaucracies, panoptic surveillance, the consolidation of technocratic hegemonies, the failures of wide-scale social engineering, and the persistence – the prevalence even – of poverty, war, famine, disease and economic exploitation in so-called 'Third world' or 'undeveloped' nations.

In the light of these failures Lyotard views Western society as marked by a wide-spread 'incredulity towards metanarratives' (PC xxiv) in the latter half of the twentieth century, and this decline in the credibility of the claims and predictions of the meta-narratives of modernity has correspondingly resulted in the proliferation of numerous smaller narratives that Lyotard refers to as 'language-games'. This is a term that Lyotard loosely borrows from Ludwig Wittgenstein as a means of accounting for the diversity of domains and modes in which people now interact. Though still narrative in form, they are no longer as stable or uniform in structure or fixed in relation to the narratorial roles they invoke (for the narrator, narratee or narrated can switch roles) as the narratives that characterised pre-literate societies. Indeed, they can overlap or even contain other games as sub-sets, due to the multiplication of specialised skills, interests and types of knowledge that striate and constitute contemporary society.

He refers to these stories as 'games' because they consist of discursive 'moves' (utterances, actions and responses) that are constrained by implicit yet binding rules and agreements amongst the player-participants concerning what is usually permissible and what constitutes a successful or winning move or strategy. More importantly, like games they involve the participants playing for 'stakes' (for access to resources or control over the outcomes) in which competing strategies and flexible manoeuvres are brought to bear (subject to a principle of *agon* (i.e. struggle) in which each tries to trump the others). Such games, however, need not involve players directly competing with one another – they can sometimes, in a sense, compete against themselves, inasmuch as they try to outdo or best their own previous moves or 'wins'.

Lyotard's key point is that these diverse games, which may overlap or be in competition for dominance of a field or discipline, constitute the weave of the social fabric or social bond (and one in which the subjectivity of the participants is itself a by-product of the strategies and outcomes of the games they play). For much the same reasons – and in a process facilitated by capitalism's purely pragmatic and instrumentalist attitude to vestigial traditions and customs – the competition within, and between, such a plurality of games makes this fabric increasingly prone to internal fragmentation. From Lyotard's perspective, however, this fragmentation is not automatically detrimental because he believes it also facilitates the potential decentralisation of power and challenges the 'givens' of existing knowledge.

The details of Lyotard's arguments about these issues need not concern us too much here. We need only acknowledge that they provide the groundwork for his subsequent claim that because the meta-narratives of modernity have increasingly become socially and politically discredited and been forced to make room for other smaller stories, so too has this fragmentation and de-centring led science (primarily the so-called 'natural' sciences but also increasingly the social sciences) to collectively shift its own allegiances and undergo a significant transformation as a result. Essentially, the convergent interests of commerce and techno-science (i.e. the way that the pursuit and practice of science has increasingly become tied to the direct application of knowledge in industrial and electronic forms), has led to a situation in which appeals to meta-narratives of progress or emancipation, and to notions of the common social 'good' or historical inevitability, are no longer necessary for justifying or grounding their efforts.

Today science, Lyotard argues, is primarily a type of language-game which immanently inter-relates, co-ordinates and facilitates the authorisation of other language-games (specific disciplines or areas of endeavour) in accordance with an identifiable method that is premised upon specific kinds of verifiable, discursive claims. However, the depreciation of the meta-narratives to which it had previously made appeal from the eighteenth century up until the mid-twentieth century has forced it to base its legitimacy on some other, less monolithic foundation devoid of appeals to transcendence.

Lyotard argues that science has sought to sustain itself through three distinct yet interrelated strategies: i) by privileging or valuing only one type of discursive formation above all others: denotative statements (i.e. objective, verifiable claims of the type 'X is the case' or 'X is not the case'); ii) through claiming to be independent of or superior to narrative, which it otherwise dismisses as illegitimate and unfounded opinion (whilst nonetheless making repeated calls upon narrative – for example, the story of the 'big bang', the theory of evolution, the history of how mathematics develops, the story of how an isotope decays, and so forth – when it has to account for itself to other disciplines or society at large for economic or pedagogical purposes); and most importantly iii) by grounding itself in a principle of 'performativity' or pragmatics (i.e. concerning what 'works' and provides identifiable results). Instead of a prevailing meta-narrative, in its place a new criterion of 'performance' is established in respect to the most efficient, efficacious and optimised realisation of specific techno-scientific goals.

This stems directly from the increasing dependence of science and scientists, and of academics more generally, on funding from state bodies (including universities) and private corporations, which in turn demand some kind of practical, and in the foreseeable long run, profitable outcome. Thus scientific research, even in its most abstract and theoretical forms, becomes cynically and mercenarily wedded to, and imbricated within capitalist commodification by way of industrialisation, computerisation, and their offspring technology, which collectively Lyotard refers to as 'development' (or 'the system'). Each scientific endeavour is obliged to deliver some kind of economically viable output (irrespective of whether its social relevance is evident or not), and thus it is subject like all capitalist business to a basic equation concerning investment and return indicative of the axiom so beloved by 'economic rationalists': minimum input must result in maximum gain. As such, efficiency, optimisation and innovation become watchwords in the directing of funding, resourcing and evaluation – for an envisaged (even if long deferred) profitable outcome overrides any actual human needs. In this way performativity dominates and unites the overall network of capitalist (and consumer) interaction and everything is consequently reduced in an 'instrumental' fashion to economic efficacy.

This new performative criterion that increasingly permeates society emphasises the optimisation of results and acceleration of productivity through the efficient (read: minimal) application of knowledge, skills and resources, and the abbreviation or marginalisation – even the culling – of time-intensive activities which are not directly profitable or which do not readily lend themselves to processes of commodification and consumption. This goes hand in hand with the focus on computerisation inasmuch as the translation of knowledge into binary code facilitates this process of optimisation, and, conversely, any form of experience that does not readily lend itself to this process is viewed as without value and gradually eliminated through a kind of conceptual 'Social Darwinism'. Failure to comply carries an implicit threat entailing 'a certain level of terror, whether soft or hard: be operational (that is, be commensurable) or disappear' (PC xxiv).

Although the scenario of performativity and efficiency that Lyotard describes seems to be a horrific and unrelentingly grim picture of dehumanisation and potential enslavement, evincing Heidegger's notion of *Gestell*, he also argues that the situation is not currently as bleak or hopeless as it first appears. The very incredulity and cynicism towards meta-narratives that pushes science into the arms of capitalism and the attendant fragmentation of the scientific 'community' which results from its being tied to specific techno-scientific goals, also simultaneously enlarges science's capacity for doubt and experimentation, and enables new possibilities. In principle science no longer owes allegiance to any given intellectual consensus or social status quo (apart from its funding agency) thus fracturing the creation of any kind of new social, economic or political unity. Also, no longer able to make appeal to an overarching meta-narrative as a means of controlling its inclusivity and exclusivity, its disciplinary and discursive boundaries become potentially more porous and tolerant towards competing paradigms, fringe endeavours, and strategic experimentation. In the light of these changes, the radical scepticism and proliferation of competing language-games, that characterise science and society in the latter half of the twentieth century, begin to make room for other possibilities along the fracture lines that criss-cross such fields of research – they provide the motor that drives investigation. It is out of these cracks that resistance and paradox increasingly emerge to challenge the dominant paradigms. The appearance of concepts such as quantum theory, catastrophe theory, chaos theory, fractals, probability theory and non-linear systems are all indicative of these changes but they are also contributors to this same transformation. Lyotard argues that as a result we see an emerging dissensus and process of destabilisation informing much contemporary scientific research, one that suggests an open-ended 'model of legitimation that has nothing to do with maximised performance, but has as its basis difference understood as paralogy' (PC 60). It enables a scenario in which in conceptual terms everything is potentially up for grabs. This emergent 'postmodern' science of paralogy (the study of paradox – or more literally in philosophy, the study of 'false thinking') that emerges from the interstices of traditional mainstream science pursues unexpected or 'bad' moves in the language-games of science and knowledge more broadly. It destabilises the 'norms' and rules that organise both the specific field and its relation to its discipline and the rest of knowledge. These moves are not innovative (that is, simply better, more stream-lined or efficacious moves within the game's existing rules and parameters) but subversive efforts that challenge the very rules of the game and in doing so redefine its boundaries, its goals and its legitimacy: not in order to modify the game, but so as to completely transform it. It is these radical moves, and the spirit of doubt, of scepticism, that compel them to challenge the existing rules and paradigms of thought, which also ultimately reveal them to be deserving of the name 'postmodern'.

Given all of the above, perhaps the most striking thing about *The Postmodern Condition* is that it says almost nothing directly about the arts. However, almost everything it does say has significant implications for the arts, inasmuch as it provides the basic coordinates – that is, that the postmodern concerns radical doubt or scepticism and that this in turn provokes unexpected 'moves' or paralogies – for Lyotard's subsequent analysis. For a discussion of these ideas and their implications in relation to the arts more specifically we now turn to 'Answering the Question: What is Postmodernism?' which was included as an appendix to the English translation of *The Postmodern Condition* but written three years after the original French version of the report.[2]

This is a far more overtly polemical piece than the earlier work. Here Lyotard throws down the gauntlet, challenging and condemning those who would seek to abolish or dilute the legacy of the artistic avant-garde and its ongoing challenge to orthodoxy. Indeed, the article begins with Lyotard's condemnation of those who would demand of artists and the arts that they collectively put an end to purportedly elitist and obscurantist experimentalism and instead become a handmaiden to social unity. In particular he singles out Jürgen Habermas, also one of his targets in *The Postmodern Condition*, as an example of such a demand for the renewal or restitution of the still unfinished emancipatory project (and meta-narrative) of modernity.

Habermas in a lecture presented in 1980 and published the following year as 'Modernity versus Postmodernity' (and again in 1983 under its better known title 'Modernity – An Incomplete Project'), is critical of the celebration of irrationalism and cynicism that he sees as overtaking Western society and which he clearly views as indicative of the work of Lyotard, although he does not name him directly. Habermas, building upon ideas drawn from his own earlier studies of communication and social theory, views the increasing specialisation of knowledge and labour throughout the last century, and the growing dominance of a particularly instrumental view of rationality indicative of modern bureaucracy, as having fragmented modern communities, increased social and economic alienation, severed social bonds, and left ordinary people at the mercy of various 'experts'. He believes that only effective communication based on the still relevant universalist principles and values of the Enlightenment (such as clarity, reason, tolerance, transparency or turn-taking) can provide a means for society to collectively address and produce a consensus able to potentially overcome the problems of ignorance, exploitation and inequality. In respect to the arts this problem is particularly acute. The efforts of the avant-garde in its original incarnation at the beginning of the twentieth century were an attempt to negotiate this situation by challenging an increasingly monolithic and stifling bourgeois world view, and offering in its place a wide diversity of means of exploring radical ideas of political change, of new social possibilities for overcoming alienation, inequality and oppression. However, the avant-garde's own broad range of activities led to a fragmentary dispersal in which its works became increasingly obscure, inaccessible and socially marginalised – dependent on experts to decode artworks and the cultural capital to enjoy them – thus exacerbating the problem of alienation. As a result, Habermas argues that the arts in the second half of the twentieth century have been marked by a retreat from these originally political and utopian aspirations into a new conservatism that embraces its own alienation. In place of this he advocates that the arts renew their commitment to exploring radical and utopian political possibilities of action and transformation in an accessible way, and bridging or healing the divisions that beset society through the construction of a new social consensus.

Unsurprisingly Lyotard dismisses such calls for consensus or unity, which he regards as the worst and most destructive kinds of palliative in contemporary culture. In a world where modernity and capitalism have overturned traditional social bonds and increasingly 'de-realised' familiar objects, experiences and institutions so that reality itself is persistently brought into question, such appeals to simplistic remedies or calls for amelioration are, he believes, a key part of the problem they purport to overcome. Thus the project of the Enlightenment is not simply incomplete but no longer coherent, and meta-narratives that promise the emancipation of the disenfranchised or the fulfilling of History or of a universal Subject are no longer tenable. Similarly Lyotard is sceptical of the disparate demands for a return to order, truth, reality, foundations, unity, or identity – all of which, he claims, converge on supressing or liquidating the experimental legacy of the avant-garde. Instead these demands, and their accompanying call for artists and writers to provide a palatable therapy for the anxiety that besets contemporary existence, mark the vestiges of a fantasy of social restoration or reintegration rendered increasingly obsolete by capitalism and modernity. Yet, Lyotard insists, this does not mean that the arts have no role to play. Indeed, the avant-garde, which is born of this very crisis – in which traditional social, political and aesthetic moorings have been broken and little can henceforth be taken for granted – is thus placed in a privileged position to confront, expose and even modulate this state of affairs.

Here, Lyotard returns to notions introduced in *Discourse, Figure* and which anticipate development in his later article

'Representation, Presentation, Unpresentable' discussed in Chapter 3. He claims that photography and cinema displace painting and literature, respectively, as pre-eminent cultural forms not just because they serve to complete the 'ordering of the visible elaborated by the Quattrocento' and thus the comprehensive mapping (or colonisation) of social experience, but also because in their attachment to and promotion of a prevalent 'realism' they are able to accomplish 'better, faster, and with a circulation a hundred thousand times larger' the fundamental task of such realism: 'to preserve various consciousnesses from doubt' (PC 74). Photography and cinema can more effectively and more efficiently sustain the consoling fantasy of shared communication and faith in a consensual reality because they are better able to 'stabilize the referent, to arrange it according to a point of view which endows it with a recognisable meaning, to reproduce the syntax and vocabulary which enable the addressee to decipher images and sequences quickly, and so to arrive at the consciousness of his own identity as well as the approval which he therefore receives from others' (PC 74). The ubiquity of photography and film make them highly effective means of sustaining the contemporary social fabric and facilitate and legitimise the circulation and address of various individual and group desires (and if proof of this claim should be required one need look no further than advertising or public relations to see this at work).

It is important to realise that what Lyotard refers to here as 'reality' is not some supposedly objective foundation for experience (the world in its bare materiality) but rather our shared values and meanings concerning that world which are shaped by 'unspoken' yet prevalent codes and conventions. In short, it is the ideological or phantasmatic construction or configuration of a shared consensual reality and, as such, its form and specific representational codes and conventions are subject to variation from one era and one culture to another. To return to an example already cited in Chapter 1, this accounts for why ancient Egyptian art, in which figures are depicted 'side-on', appears unrealistic to the contemporary observer yet would have constituted the recognisable representational currency – the 'realism' – of its original setting, for its form emblematically privileged specific meanings and values concerning social status, mythical origins, political authority, and spiritual preoccupations that we no longer share. Conversely, the dominant representations and conventions that we embrace as realistic today would not appear so to an ancient Egyptian somehow transported forward in time.

Lyotard's essential claim concerning 'reality' is that objectivity matters far less than a shared preparedness (whether conscious or not) to accept something as true or real or efficacious. Even an appeal to a 'correspondence theory' (i.e. that what we say or think is only true or real when it accurately reflects what we perceive and is thus verifiable) is constantly traversed and thus compromised by the ebb and flow of various conceptual, semantic and semiotic transformations, on the one hand, and diverse personal, social, political and cultural pressures, on the other. Social reality as such (which is the primary form through which we grasp ourselves and our world) is thus always relative to our own degree of conformity with dominant cultural representations.

However, the competing forces that mark modernity and capitalism have placed considerable pressure on the viable and seamless construction and maintenance of such a unified social framework (as we saw Lyotard describe in *The Postmodern Condition* in relation to language-games) – indeed, it is constantly under threat of being exposed as a kind of consensual fiction. This threat of the unreality of 'reality' constitutes a crisis for contemporary society that it continually seeks to deny, one that presents a particular issue for the arts of painting and literature that goes beyond their seeming obsolescence in the face of the encroachments of more recent technological forms (and indeed poses a problem for any medium or work that wishes to call itself 'art'): namely, that their own marginalisation invites a questioning of their support (both materially and ideologically) of this dominant 'reality'. As practices that traditionally purported to depict various aspects or levels of experience, painting and literature are hereafter forced to confront their own complicity with the processes that seduce and deceive society and to choose between continuing down this path (as part of the existing 'culture industry' – i.e. the mass media and its related technologies – which promotes and prescribes conformity to a certain set of expectations or determinate rules and judgements concerning what is reality and the non-threatening ways in which it should be represented) or of refusing, and even challenging, its aims and demands. To embrace the first path individually rewards those who would produce cultural works whilst divesting those same works of any critical significance (lest it threaten their marketability), whilst the second unsurprisingly leads to further social and economic marginalisation. However, the latter path also frees artists and the contemporary arts from the obligation to please, placate or reassure their audiences, or to accord with notions of public taste or accountability. They are thereafter free to explore and to deconstruct, in principle without fear or favour, the production of such a 'reality' through a sustained and unrelenting questioning of the accepted rules, codes and conventions that otherwise sustain it. Through a series of challenging and transforming 'bad' moves, to use the terminology of *The Postmodern Condition*, artists trump the demands of convention and consensus:

> When Cézanne takes up his brush, the stakes of painting are questioned; when Schoenberg is before his piano, so are the stakes of music; when Joyce takes hold of his pen, those of literature. Not simply new strategies for 'winning' are tried out, but the nature of 'success' is questioned... (DIFF 139)

In the face of these challenges the modern aesthetic question which gives birth to the avant-garde then becomes 'not "What is beautiful?" but "What can be said to be art (and literature)?"' – a question, as we saw in the last chapter, better suited to the sublime, an experience marked by an ambivalent and anxious feeling generated by the imagination's failure 'to present an object which, might if only in principle, come to match a concept' (PC 78). In such a sublime encounter we have an Idea of something that exceeds or subverts the limits of human knowledge and experience yet we simultaneously lack any 'capacity to show an example of it', to present a sensible counterpart for it, and so it imparts 'no knowledge about reality'. Moreover, it serves to prevent 'the free union of the faculties which give rise to the sentiment of the beautiful; and [thus prevents] the formation and stabilisation of taste' (PC 78).

Lyotard claims that the extensive interest in the sublime displayed by artists and philosophers at the end of the eighteenth century (and then again from the early twentieth century onwards) marks an important response to the intense anxiety which arises from, and yet which also undermines, modernity's attempts at denying the unreality that increasingly confronts it. In this sense, the sublime, particularly in its theorisation by Burke and Kant, anticipates aspects of Nietzsche's account of nihilism, of the de-stablisation and fragmentation of meaning that the awareness of the 'lack of reality' in reality engenders in Western culture. Indeed, the recent emergence of the avant-garde and its ongoing investigation of the 'unpresentable' is itself a symptom of nihilism (inasmuch as it serves to extend the corrosive process of doubt) but, in pushing perception and knowledge to their limits through its diverse exploratory, ground-clearing activities, the avant-garde also provides a crucial means of engaging with and modulating this same condition. Moreover, Lyotard suggests – and this signals how far he has moved away by this point from the libidinal and his earlier Nietzschean affiliations – that the concept of the sublime is perhaps less encumbered by metaphysical baggage than the notion of nihilism, because its attentions are directed primarily towards examining the experience of this 'lack of reality' in reality, of the de-realisation that characterises modernity, rather than the social and ethical devaluations that have resulted from it.

The avant-garde, in its refusal of the demands of the mainstream or of providing reassurance concerning the 'real', is caught up (whether it knows it or not) in presenting 'the fact that the unpresentable exists' and thus in making 'visible that there is something which can be conceived and which can neither be seen nor made visible'. Moreover, it pursues this in the only ways remaining to it: through allusion and indirection. Kant had already signalled this path through his insistence that 'formlessness' and 'abstraction' provide a 'negative presentation' of the unpresentable, thus soliciting its power whilst respecting its mystery. In regard to avant-garde painting (and the other experimental arts, including literature and theatre) it will '"present" something though negatively; it will therefore avoid figuration or representation...it will enable us to see only by making it impossible to see; it will please only by causing pain' (PC 78).

It is within the context of this furtherance of the process of de-realisation, of the withdrawal of the real, implicit within modernity that we are finally able to define the relationship of the avant-garde to the modern and the postmodern. But not the postmodern as it is so often characterised as a pervasive postmodern*ist* eclecticism of styles and techniques and the narcissistic freedom to choose which related commodity to consume. This Lyotard dismisses as antithetical to the project of the avant-garde; it is instead the 'realism' of the capitalist marketplace. Such eclecticism 'is the degree zero of contemporary general culture: one listens to reggae, watches a western, eats McDonald's food for lunch...[and] this realism of the "anything goes" is in fact that of money; in the absence of aesthetic criteria, it remains possible and useful to assess the value of works according to the profits they yield. Such realism accommodates all tendencies...' (PC 76).

In contrast, for Lyotard, the modern and the postmodern are, in fact, different modalities of the sublime encounter with modernity, depending on whether the emphasis is placed, in the case of the former, upon the painful failure of matching the presentable to the conceivable and the sense of impotence, inadequacy and grief that this induces, or in the latter, on the pleasurable exuberance and surprise which provokes us to discover or invent new moves and new rules of the 'game'. The first of these marks the modern, the second the postmodern. The first clings desperately to the shattered remnants of a disappearing or elusive 'real', the other joyfully abandons it. The first somehow believes that the unities (or a priori nature) of time and space can provide a bulwark or defence against the loss of meaning and certitude, whereas the other no longer concerns itself with them.

As an example, Lyotard draws a contrast between the key works of Marcel Proust and James Joyce. The former's *A la recherche du temps perdu* (usually translated as *Remembrance of Things Past* but more accurately, *In Search of Lost Time*) recounts the inevitable and irretrievable losses implicit in the temporality of a lived life yet which despite itself continually attempts to reconstitute and reintegrate these events and recollections through the unifying consciousness of the narrator Marcel (that it is *his* life) and the narrative's own circular form (that Marcel's journey leads him to 'write' the book that we are reading). Thus the *form* of the work provides a relatively coherent pseudo-unity that disavows the fragmentation or dispersal implicit in what it depicts, and which, amid the unravelling conventions of narrative and representation, still searches for the basic temporal and spatial co-ordinates that might yet negotiate any loss of meaning inherent in the work (PC 80).

In the case of Joyce, however, we find instead in *Ulysses,* and even more so in *Finnegans Wake*, an overturning of all the established rules and givens, which 'allows the unpresentable to become perceptible in his writing, in the signifier' and where 'the whole range of available narrative and even stylistic operators is put into play *without concern for the unity of the whole*' (emphasis added; PC 82). Here then is the difference between a sublime response that surrenders itself to what it initially sought to escape or overcome and a more defiant, reckless embrace of the unknown:

> [For] modern aesthetics is an aesthetic of the sublime, though a nostalgic one. It allows the unpresentable to be put forward only as the missing contents; but the form, because of its recognisable consistency, continues to offer to the reader or viewer matter for solace and pleasure...[whereas the postmodern is] that which, in the modern, puts forward the unpresentable in presentation itself; that which denies itself the solace of good forms, the consensus of a taste which would make it possible to share collectively the nostalgia for the unattainable; that which searches for new presentations, not in order to enjoy them but in order to impart a stronger sense of the unpresentable. (PC 81)

Moreover, although these two modes are linked to different aspects of the sublime, they 'often co-exist in the same piece, are almost indistinguishable; and yet they testify to a difference on which the fate of thought depends and will depend for a long time, between regret and assay' (PC 80). In a manner that evokes Lyotard's earlier discussions of Freud's account of the life and death drives, these contrary impulses struggle for primacy in the work and its reception. However, it is the postmodern as an unrelenting questioning of what has come before that ultimately provides the internal motor for change and renewal, continually challenging the modern to exceed its own melancholic inertia: 'A work can become modern only if it is first postmodern. Postmodernism thus understood is not modernism at its end but in the nascent state, and this state is constant.'

Although both modern and postmodern works of art attempt to challenge or question consensual 'reality' by alluding to that which cannot be perceived, or by foregrounding the fact that something is unpresentable, the modern work, Lyotard claims, is nonetheless inclined to fall back into the consoling embrace of the 'real', even if in a form initially remote from the quotidian. Unlike those postmodern works that suspend, destabilise or even eviscerate the notion of the 'real', modern works strive to dilate the boundaries of the latter in order to encompass and thereby govern whatever unfamiliar, hidden or irreconcilable elements they confront. Indeed, through this latter process of colonising experience, and their own subsequent domestication and petrification by way of the academy, 'cultural tourism' and the mass media, modern works often come to provide a support, if not the basis, for a new (more up to date) and expansive 'realism'. In contrast, in striving to resist these same processes of colonisation and assimilation the postmodern artist or writer is placed in a position analogous to a philosopher, for the works that he or she produces

> are not in principle governed by pre-established rules, and they cannot be judged according to a determinate judgement, by applying familiar categories to the text or to the work. Those rules and categories are what the work of art itself is looking for. The artist and the writer, then, are working without rules in order to formulate the rules of what *will have been done*. (PC 81)

In his conclusion, Lyotard reiterates his view that it is not the place of artists to supply or shore up the fantasy of reality or to console those who mourn its disappearance – for in that direction lies the terror that conformity imposes on its subjects, a price already paid many times over throughout the nineteenth and twentieth centuries – but to invent new 'allusions to the conceivable which cannot be presented'.

If *The Postmodern Condition* provided an introduction to Lyotard's theorising of the postmodern and its relevance to science, and 'Answering the Question: What is Postmodernism?' more specifically linked the postmodern to the arts and an aesthetics of the sublime, then in 'Rewriting Modernity' we find Lyotard providing a speculative and reflexive commentary on his own theorising of the postmodern and its relation to his broader philosophical project.

Based on a lecture given in 1986 and published the following year, the article already states in its title Lyotard's aim in *The Postmodern Condition* and its appendix, as well as the numerous articles published in its wake: of reworking our understanding of modernity. Putting to one side for the moment the ambiguities attached to the word 'rewriting' that Lyotard will subsequently explore, we should note that in refraining from using the term 'postmodern' in preference for 'modernity' in the title, he claims this has the advantage of deflecting attention away from whatever confusions initially beset the prefix 'post', whilst still allowing the core issues concerning the postmodern and its relation to modernity to be examined and foregrounded. Moreover, the replacement of 'post' with the 're' of *rewriting* retains an emphasis on the notion that temporality is somehow still at stake, that something is occurring in relation to (and within) modernity and that this is a matter that cannot be settled without re-examination and revision. Together, Lyotard claims, these two shifts in the title, syntactical and lexical, mark a 'double displacement' (INH 24) – a phrase that harks back to the 'double reversal' described in *Discourse, Figure* 15 years earlier.

More importantly, for Lyotard, this double displacement sidesteps many of the difficulties attendant on viewing modernity and the postmodern in terms of periodisation, of a 'before' and 'after', in particular, periodisation's failure to account for (or even acknowledge) the problem of the 'now', obscuring instead what is already presumed in such chronology: namely, one's own position. Lyotard links this to a long-standing concern in philosophy, whose most famous exemplar, Aristotle, noted the difficulty of defining, from within the flow of time, the present in respect to what has been or will be. The 'now' is amorphous or indeterminate, for when we reach for it we find either it has not yet arrived or is already gone. Lyotard similarly asserts that our inability to delimit the temporal 'now' constitutes an excess wherein what we experience is both too soon and too late in respect to our understanding of what has occurred (an idea also evident in his writings on Newman's paintings). He adds that when we apply this perspective to modernity (to the modern and the postmodern) it highlights the problems inherent in viewing them in terms of periodisation, with the result that they can no longer simply be 'identified and defined as clearly circumscribed historical entities' in a process of succession. Essentially this concern with periodisation, of the 'pre' and 'post', leaves out the question of the very place and time from which one presumes to legitimately speak of these matters (as if one was 'outside' or transcendent to this process of chronological mapping).

This is further complicated, Lyotard argues, by the fact that the postmodern is already 'implied' or present within modernity because the latter comprises an internal 'impulsion or desire to exceed itself into a state other than itself' (INH 26) and thereafter to seek a final and enduring state of stability. In striving to escape itself and the past, modernity is marked both by dissatisfaction (or anxiety) and a simultaneous wish to overcome the former (modulated as a corresponding confrontation with its own condition and its attempt to flee from it). In this regard 'postmodernity' can move in either one of two directions: as modernity's attempted realisation of its self-evasions and phantasies of emancipation (postmodern*ism*) or as an interrogation of its underlying desires and self-mythologising (the postmodern). As we have seen in *The Postmodern Condition* and 'Answering the Question: What is Postmodernism?' modernity already encompasses diverse responses to the 'lack of reality' in reality that it produces: in the case of the former it posits the postmodern as an internal process of radical questioning that undermines both meta-narratives and the status quo, and in the latter, it presents the modern as an attempted negotiation of this lack and the postmodern as the embrace of the aporia it constitutes. But in both cases the postmodern is a modality of modernity and in this sense, Lyotard adds, modernity is 'constitutionally and ceaselessly pregnant with its postmodernity' (INH 25).

Lyotard introduces here another crucial point, and one partly anticipated seven years before in *Just Gaming*, that, as a result of their mutual imbrication, modernity and the postmodern can no longer be viewed as directly opposed to one another. Instead modernity opposes itself to the 'Classical', a way of thinking and of 'being' characterised by a mythic conception of time as rhythmic and rhyming, that is as cyclical and resistant to linear change, in which time or history constitutes a complete and unbroken movement or unity of meaning, and beginning and end match or complement one another in a pre-destined fashion.

Unlike the Classical, modernity, because of its desire to exceed itself, is obsessed with historical periodisation (as proof of its own efforts, successes and failures) and of compulsively dating these divisions and transitions. It envisages time as a broken unity divided into separate, successive blocks, marked by a sense of beginnings (of inaugurating something 'new') and of endings (of restarting the clock from zero but in a new, different era), but also as a fragmentation that aspires to re-integration at a higher level (as meta-narrative). In essence, modernity repeatedly attempts to write its own history and in doing so to *rewrite* it: 'In Christianity, Cartesianism or Jacobinism, this same gesture designates a Year One, that of revolution and redemption in the one case, of rebirth and renewal in the second, or again of revolution and reappropriation of liberties' (INH 25–26).

In addressing this issue Lyotard emphasises the ambiguity of the 're-' of the rewriting referred to in his article's title – not in order to signal a return to a beginning or inaugurate yet another era or point of revolution or renewal but rather to mark a different kind of re-writing in which modernity does not, and *cannot*, escape from itself in search of rebirth or redemption. Instead it is forced into a constant process of re-view, re-visitation and self-excavation that Lyotard calls the 'postmodern', and although the latter is characterised by a persistent pushing at the boundaries and questioning of our beliefs and expectations (and a potential rewriting of the rules that guide our thinking or behaviour), it is inherently related to modernity as a kind of 'figure' that troubles and challenges it from within.

In 'Rewriting Modernity' Lyotard likens this process of re-examination to the psychoanalytic concept of *Durcharbeiten* – of a 'working through' or a 'working over' of the hidden or repressed aspects of something – a notion drawn from a short yet important piece by Freud on psychoanalytic technique. In this article 'Repeating, Remembering and Working Through', Freud distinguishes between the three modes of engagement with unconscious processes in therapeutic practice signalled by the paper's title.

The first of these processes, repetition, characterises the general workings of neurosis and psychosis that organise unconscious desire in the form of a 'set-up' (dispositif). In this set-up the individual's existence is lived in accordance with an unconscious script that they helplessly and compulsively re-enact over and over again. It is a phantasmatic scenario that ensures a destiny in which everything is (psychically) determined in advance, despite the patient's attempts (like tragic Oedipus) to evade its outcome (INH 26–27).

In psychoanalytic treatment, however, patients are encouraged to explore and discover, through the recollection of dreams or remembrances of their past experiences, the reasons or motives for their pre-destined and oppressive sufferings (their repetitive thoughts, behaviours, symptoms) so as to potentially break with the self-destructive cycle that constitutes this 'inescapable' fate. However, this desire to find the real cause of their trauma, and the congruent belief that such a cause can be identified, recovered and purged, presents its own problems. For in remembering one wants, much like a detective, to identify the facts of the 'crime', to locate the original motive or unveil the truth, yet this desire is itself already caught up with or entrenched within the fulfilling of this destiny, of the narrative that is woven from it. Basically, the belief in an origin or a ground, on the one hand, and of emancipation from its dictates, on the other, already renders one complicit with the organising phantasy (in this case, of believing that there is both a specific reason and a cure for one's suffering). However, striving to escape the past by identifying its faults does not necessarily prevent one from re-enacting those same mistakes and this trap extends far beyond the province of the analyst's couch, as Lyotard demonstrates with the example of Nietzsche. In seeking to emancipate us from metaphysics and to demonstrate that its claims to provide an origin or ground are illusory, Nietzsche ultimately became caught in this same trap. For having exposed the metaphysical underpinnings of Western culture he then 'succumbed to the temptation' of positing a grounding principle for his own philosophy – namely, the 'will to power' – and thus reinstalling the same metaphysical principles that he sought to overcome (INH 28–29).

As Lyotard observes, it is in this sense of 'remembering', as recovery and then emancipation or transcendence, that a concern with modernity (and thus with modern*ism* and postmodern*ism* as conventionally understood) is usually undertaken or enacted – of exposing a closed destiny and opening it up to something supposedly new and liberating (the possibility of rebirth or renewal or redemption and thus of escaping one's destiny or past crimes). However, he cautions that viewing the act of recollection in and of itself as a means of providing a cure or answer is to fall into the trap of an obsession with origins and beginnings, of a temporality sub-divided and organised accorded to chronology or periodisation, and thus of the very ethos from which one seeks escape – that in fleeing one's destiny one potentially and unconsciously re-inscribes it in another form:

> Far from really rewriting it, supposing this to be possible, all one is doing is writing again, and making real modernity itself. The point being that writing it is always rewriting it. Modernity is written, inscribes itself on itself, in a perpetual rewriting. (INH 28)

But not all forms of rewriting within modernity are equivalent. This form of rewriting as a kind of 'remembering' (which finally forgets that it is a *re*-writing) potentially commits the same errors, the same crimes, at a different level: for remembering is in fact a way of forgetting the ongoing anxiety one faces by attributing it to an identifiable fault. It is a determinate rewriting that has a specific departure and destination in view, and which disavows or disowns its own investments, its own phantasies.

In contrast, 'working through' as a kind of anamnesis constitutes a different kind of rewriting, distinguishable from this remembering that already presupposes its own amnesia (that in recollecting something we also come to forget the act of previously having forgotten it). In 'working through' in the therapeutic situation, the analyst encourages the patient to move beyond simply *re*-membering, and thus re-organising the past in to a new narrative drawn from the same elements or a meta-narrative that subordinates them. In part this involves a preparedness to forego belief in a definitive first cause, an empirical or objective origin. As Lyotard notes, it was only when Freud relinquished the so-called 'seduction theory', his belief that the origin of neurosis, its 'primal scene', stemmed from an objective traumatic cause or empirical occurrence (and moreover, an event that was retrievable by consciousness), that he was able to fully develop the notion of the unconscious (INH 30). Thereafter Freud came to see that this supposed origin was in fact a retroactive effect (*Nachträglichkeit*) which imbued previous elements with a significance and causal efficacy that they previously lacked, and was woven from the back-and-forth movement between fragments of past and present concerns. In turn, this absence of an origin led Freud to speculate that the analytic encounter was devoid of a readily predictable or identifiable conclusion, thus making treatment – as a 'working through' of psychic content – potentially interminable: 'Contrary to remembering, working thorough would be defined as a work without end and therefore without will: without end in the sense in which it is not guided by the concept of an end – but not without finality' (INH 30).

Notably, this analytic 'working through' required a special approach to the psychic material it encountered: on the part of the patient it required a commitment to 'free association', of resisting the compulsion to either impose censorship on the flow and articulation of thought and feeling or of pre-judging the meaning of whatever presented itself; and on the part of the analyst, it demanded a complementary cultivation of 'free-floating' attention, a receptivity towards all material (no matter how seemingly trivial), that involved suspension of judgement and a preparedness to follow wherever such associative links might lead (INH 30).

Interestingly, Lyotard suggests that in its use of suspended attention and free association in pursuit of emancipation from neurotic suffering, Freud's therapeutic treatment bears some resemblance to Kant's notion of the 'reflective' aesthetic judgement – at least in respect of the beautiful: that it promotes a contemplation of the material raised, devoid of pre-existing concepts, with the aim of seeking a potential harmony of the faculties or a reduction of cognitive dissonance that will enable the patient to (re)commit to social integration (INH 33). In this regard, even though Freud refrains from promising a 'cure' he still seeks to bring about a transition and a stabilisation in the patient's psyche.

At first glance the initial stages of the 'working through' of modernity involves something akin to the Freudian notion of suspended judgement, that Lyotard calls 'passability' – an open-ended receptivity that does not automatically impose meanings on events, giving itself over to them instead in an exploratory way. In this manner one approaches or receives the fragments of experience – a thought, a feeling, a colour, a scrap of information, an activity, a phrase – embracing each without pre-judging it, and bringing them gradually into resonant contact with one another without the pre-imposition of reason, hierarchy or mediation. We cannot say in advance (because we do not yet know) what is important in these encounters or how their elements might be linked and even what will take place or is taking place. Yet passability is not chained to the prospect of an emancipatory desire. As Lyotard notes – drawing an important distinction between the Freudian use of 'working through', which is circumscribed by its clinical setting and hence the aim of alleviating the patient's suffering (an emancipation from the tyranny of the symptom or at least reconciling of the patient with its least destructive demands), and of how it might apply in the case of modernity – the passability of the postmodern encounter with modernity does not have liberation or reconciliation as its goal. Indeed it questions the assumptions underlying this attempt to flee from the 'lack of reality' in reality, demonstrating a preparedness to confront the anguish of not knowing what is being experienced and the potentially interminable nature of this undertaking.

This also highlights the crucial issue of 'suffering' that marks the division between these two notions of 'working through'. Undeniably, the therapeutic approach is, despite its 'reflective' character and its emancipatory aspirations, continually confronted by the almost intolerable suffering that a patient endures, and the persistent difficulty, in the absence of an easily identifiable empirical cause, of dealing with this ongoing trauma. In addressing this, Freud in his later work speculates that although there is no specific, locatable cause or original event that produces neurosis, the patient's symptomatic behaviour, the general outline of his or her various repressions, seems organised around an enigmatic and inaccessible kernel – a kind of formless, non-origin that Freud refers to as 'primary repression', and which resides beyond even the phantasy of the 'primal scene'. This notion was taken up and developed by Lacan, who linked it to the irretrievable 'lost object' that he called 'the Thing' (*das Ding*), and which provided in part the basis for Lyotard's notion of the figure-matrix, as we saw in Chapter 1.

This unconscious kernel – as an absence invested retroactively with power and significance – insists within the subject's psyche as an unsymbolisable and unimaginable element. In the analytic process of 'working through' it is approached though the ongoing examination of repetition and recollection yet it can never be reached or confronted directly or even laid to rest because it is constitutively unpresentable. As such it poses a radical heterogeneity that resists the reconciliation of consciousness with the unconscious, and threatens to subvert or derail the analytic cure by dispossessing the subject of the self-knowledge, the self-certainty or stability that it craves.

This description of something in analysis that is both unpresentable and un-finalisable strikingly evokes the works and efforts of the avant-garde, which as we have seen are dedicated to exploring and presenting sublime allusions. Unsurprisingly, the unpresentability of primary repression or the 'Thing' conjures for Lyotard the indeterminate and 'formless' sublime, an encounter that he views as an inherently spectral and deferred potential within the Freudian therapeutic scenario. Indeed, Lyotard draws a direct analogy between the sublime and primary repression (the unknowable and irretrievable seed), distinguishing the latter from the secondary repressions (the withholding from consciousness of specific unacceptable ideas or feelings) that constitute the primary raw material of therapeutic recollection. Like the sublime, primary repression can never be presented in itself, merely alluded to indirectly, leading Lyotard to conclude in developing this parallel that 'Primary repression…would thus be to secondary repression what the sublime is to the beautiful' (INH 33).[3]

In respect to modernity we can analogously distinguish between a kind of 'unpresentable' primary repression or 'Thing' and secondary repression (the specific cultural 'memories' and occurrences that preoccupy much of the academy and culture industry). The former haunts thought and '"language", the tradition and the material with, against and in which it writes' (INH 33), both making possible and simultaneously undoing the consensus through which contemporary society understands itself and its aspirations. In this regard, it is closely related to the effects of the 'lack of reality' that modernity engenders within reality and yet which modernity otherwise displaces or disowns through the promise of meta-narratives of transcendence and emancipation, or the promotion of a 'realism' that 'protects consciousness from doubt', or the 'nostalgia for the unattainable' that frames the aesthetic of the modern. In contrast, the 'Thing' is that which disfigures from within modernity its attempts to both exceed and fulfil itself; it is that same sense of something 'unpresentable' to which the avant-garde has dedicated its endeavours.

We should note, however, that in regard to this modified notion of 'working through' – as a receptivity towards something unconscious that is fundamentally unpresentable and yet constitutive – and its application to modernity, Lyotard emphasises two crucial features that distance it from its psychoanalytic cousin. These are acknowledgements that, firstly, this process can give us no real knowledge of the past or of history as such (indeed it refuses the synthesis of temporality and narrative that we usually call a 'life' or a 'culture' or an 'era') and, secondly, that it cannot, and should not aspire to, alleviate or filter out the suffering, the painful dissonance, that arises from the sublime encounter with something unpresentable. This modified notion of rewriting or 'working through' which Lyotard calls 'perlaboration', when applied to modernity, recasts the postmodern as something far removed from the compulsive repetition and recollection of culture as quotation, eclecticism, parody and recycling that typifies contemporary society, or as the product of technologies which seek to predetermine our experiences in non-threatening forms (i.e. the new beautiful).

Lyotard deploys his 'postmodern' rewriting of modernity as a means of challenging the latter's self-delusions, its complicity with capitalist techno-science, and its attempts at escaping its own contradictory desires. As such, the postmodern does not present a break with the past or the promise of a utopian future but the working through of an ongoing and multi-layered heritage, a different way of reflecting upon events:

> Postmodernity is not a new age, but the rewriting of some of the features claimed by modernity, and first of all modernity's claim to ground its legitimacy on the ground of liberating humanity as a whole through science and technology...[it is a] rewriting that has been at work, for a long time now, in modernity itself. (INH 34)

It is in this sense of a continuous commitment to working though our contemporary condition (aesthetically, culturally, socially, politically, economically), without a pre-existing schema or end-point, that Lyotard's work retains its vitality and viability as a philosophical force, as a call to arms and a declaration of war on 'totality' – indeed, as the philosophical equivalent of the avant-garde's artistic and literary explorations of the 'unpresentable'. This examination of what remains unsaid or unseen, and more importantly of what can never be said or made visible, is the obligation, the political and ethical demand, to which he increasingly dedicated his life and thought. If Lyotard's name then is to be forever yoked to the 'postmodern' we should at least allow this legacy to stand – not as the historical headstone of a defunct theory or 'art movement', or as a sop to intellectual fashion – but as he envisaged it: as bearing witness to difference and the unpresentable through the incessant and inexhaustible re-writing of modernity.

Notes

Introduction

1 On the first anniversary of 9/11, the British artist Damien Hirst made similar remarks which were widely reported in the media and on the internet: 'You've got to hand it to them on some level because they've achieved something which nobody would have ever have thought possible – especially to a country as big as America. So on one level they kind of need congratulating, which a lot of people shy away from, which is a very dangerous thing. The thing about 9/11 is that it's kind of an artwork in its own right. It was wicked, but it was devised in this way for this kind of impact.' Hirst subsequently retracted his comments in the face of public outrage.

Chapter 1

1 This three-step manoeuvre will seem familiar perhaps to readers of the early work of Derrida on speech and writing: that is, to initially identify the binary opposition, then reverse the priority of terms, and finally to displace and subvert the relation itself in respect to a 'non-conceptual' *différance*. Indeed, this methodological 'resemblance' provides the basis for Rodolphe Gasché's dubious claim that Lyotard's efforts are closely aligned with Derrida's deconstructive (or grammatological) project (see Gasché 1994: 22–57). We should be cautious, however, about too readily conflating Lyotard's concerns with Derrida's own as, despite his use of the term 'deconstruction' (which at the time that he was writing was not so exclusively identified with Derrida's aims and philosophy), Lyotard was highly critical of aspects of Derrida's work, viewing the latter's account of signification and *arche-writing* as still too dependent upon elements imported from semiology and linguistics.

2 As Lyotard notes: 'One cannot at all say that the line which Klee's pencil traces on a sheet of paper is charged with effects of meaning in the same way as the letters which he writes under this line and which say simply: "fatal leap"' (DW 28).

3 An obvious example of how such a transformation of text into something more pictorial shifts the focus away from the transparency of reading to a figural seeing, from signification to a palpable contact with the eye, is the Medieval 'illuminated manuscript' with its decorative lettering and marginalia.

4 We should not confuse Lyotard's use of 'figural' (or sometimes even 'figure') with the 'figurative', a term employed in art history to describe the mimetic depiction of objects (either in respect to the form or outline or contour of an object, or a recognisable likeness such as the human body in portraiture).

Chapter 2

1 Lyotard provides a concise example of this structure: 'Take two places A and B; a move from A to B means two positions and a displacement; now declare that B comes from A; you are no longer taking B's position positively, affirmatively, but in relation to A, subordinated to A, itself, absent (gone by, hidden). B is turned into nothingness; as an illusion of presence, its being is in A; and A is affirmed as truth, that is to say absence' (DW 10).

Chapter 3

1 It has been pointed out by commentators that the usual French translation for the German term *Gestell* is 'dispositif', the very same word that Lyotard employs to describe energetic set-ups. See, for example, Iverson & Melville (2010: 179).

Chapter 4

1 One of the criticisms repeatedly levelled at *The Postmodern Condition* is the claim that Lyotard naively falls into the trap of constructing his own meta-narrative about the 'decline of meta-narratives'. Given his definition of a meta-narrative as organising other narratives in respect to bringing about an envisaged utopian or *telic* outcome, it should be obvious then that this criticism is invalid, as Lyotard does not posit the decline of meta-narratives in respect to any such outcome. In fact, refraining from predicting such finality is crucial to his approach.

2 Note the slightly misleading translation of the paper's title. The original title refers to the 'postmodern' and not to postmodernism. Fortunately, this is corrected in the translation included in *The Postmodern Explained to Children*.

3 This analogy is more fully developed in Lyotard's *Heidegger and "the Jews"*.

Select bibliography

To refer to the extended Recommended Reading,
visit www.ibtauris.com/lyotardreframed

Appignanesi, Lisa (1989) *Postmodernism: ICA Documents*, London: Free Association Books.

Bamford, Kif (2012) *Lyotard and the Figural in Performance, Art and Writing*, London: Continuum.

Bennington, Geoffrey (1988) *Lyotard: Writing the Event*, Manchester: Manchester University Press.

Bertens, Hans (1995) *The Idea of the Postmodern: A History*, London: Routledge.

Best, Steven and Douglas Kellner (1991) *Postmodern Theory: Critical Interrogations*, London: Macmillan.

Bolt, Barbara (2011) *Heidegger Reframed*, London: I.B.Tauris.

Bowie, Malcolm (1991) *Lacan*, Cambridge, MA: Harvard University Press.

Braver, Lee (2009) *Heidegger's Later Writings: A Reader's Guide*, London: Continuum.

Burke, Edmund (1958) *A Philosophical Enquiry into the Origin of our Ideas of the Sublime and the Beautiful*, London: Routledge & Kegan Paul.

Carroll, David (1987) *Paraesthetics: Foucault, Lyotard, Derrida*, London: Methuen.

Cazeaux, Clive (ed.) (2000) *Continental Aesthetics Reader*, London and New York: Routledge.

Choat, Simon (2010) *Marx Through Post-Structuralism*, London: Continuum.

Deleuze, Gilles (1994) *Difference and Repetition*, trans. Paul Patton, New York: Columbia University Press.

— and Félix Guattari (1983) *Anti-Oedipus*, trans. Robert Hurley, Mark Seem and Helen R. Lane, Minneapolis, MN: University of Minnesota Press.

Derrida, Jacques (1976) *Of Grammatology*, trans. Gayatari Chakravorty Spivak, Baltimore, MD: Johns Hopkins University Press.

— (1978) *Writing and Difference*, trans. Alan Bass, Chicago: University of Chicago Press.

Dews, Peter (1987) *Logics of Disintegration: Poststructuralist Thought and the Claims of Critical Theory*, London: Verso.

Foster, Hal (ed.) (1983) *The Anti-Aesthetic: Essays on Postmodern Culture*, Port Townsend, WA: Bay Press.

Foucault, Michel (1970) *The Order of Things: An Archaeology of the Human Sciences*, London: Routledge.

Freud, Sigmund (1953–1975) *The Standard Edition of the Complete Psychological Works of Sigmund Freud*, trans. James Strachey et al., London: Hogarth Press.

Gasché, Rodolphe (1994), *Inventions of Difference*, Cambridge, MA: Harvard University Press.

Habermas, Jürgen (1983) 'Modernity – an incomplete project' in *The Anti-Aesthetic: Essays on Postmodern Culture*, Hal Foster (ed.), Port Townsend, WA: Bay Press.

Harries, Karsten (2009) *Art Matters: A Critical Commentary on Heidegger's 'The Origin of the Work of Art'*, New Haven, CT: Springer.

Heidegger, Martin (1962) *Being and Time*, trans. John Macquarrie and Edward Robinson, New York: Harper and Row.

— (1977) *The Question Concerning Technology and Other Essays*, trans. William Lovitt, New York: Harper and Row, pp.3–35, 115–54.

— (2002) 'On the Origin of the Work of Art' in *Basic Writings*, trans. David Farrell Krell, London: Routledge, pp.139–212.

Hughes, Fiona (2010) *Kant's Critique of Aesthetic Judgement: A Reader's Guide*, London: Continuum.

Iverson, Margaret and Stephen Melville (2010) *Writing Art History: Disciplinary Departures*, Chicago: University of Chicago Press.

Jameson, Fredric (1983) 'Postmodernism and the consumer society' in *Postmodern Culture*, Hal Foster (ed.), Port Townsend, WA: Bay Press.

Jenks, Charles (1986) *What is Post-Modernism?* London: Art and Design.

Johnson, Galen A. (1993) *The Merleau-Ponty Aesthetics Reader: Philosophy and Painting*, Evanston, IL: Northwestern University Press.

Jones, Graham (2007) '"Look how I forget you; look how I have forgotten you!": *Hiroshima Mon Amour* and the Lyotardian sublime' in *Sensorium: Aesthetics, Art, Life*, Barbara Bolt et al. (eds), Newcastle: Cambridge Scholars Publishing.

— and Jon Roffe (eds) (2009) *Deleuze's Philosophical Lineage*, Edinburgh: Edinburgh University Press.

Kant, Immanuel (1961) *Critique of Judgement*, trans. James Creed Meredith, Oxford: Clarendon Press.

— (1997) *Critique of Practical Reason*, New York: Cambridge University Press.

— (1999) *Critique of Pure Reason*, trans. Paul Guyer and Allen W. Wood (eds), Cambridge: Cambridge University Press.

Kelly, Michael (1998) *Encyclopedia of Aesthetics,* Volume 4, Oxford: Oxford University Press.

Lacan, Jacques (1977) *The Four Fundamental Concepts of Psycho-analysis*, Jacques-Alain Miller (ed.), trans. Alain Sheridan, London: Hogarth Press.

— (2006) *Ecrits: The First Complete Edition in English*, trans. Bruce Fink et al., New York: W.W. Norton & Co.

Lyotard, Jean-François (1984) *Driftworks*, trans. Roger McKeon et al., New York: Semiotext(e).

— (1984) *The Postmodern Condition: A Report on Knowledge*, trans. Geoffrey Bennington and Brian Massumi, Manchester: Manchester University Press.

— (1988) *The Differend: Phrases in Dispute*, trans. Georges Van Den Abbeele, Manchester: Manchester University Press.

— (1989) *The Lyotard Reader*, ed. Andrew Benjamin, Oxford: Blackwell.

— (1990) *Duchamp's TRANS/formers*, trans. I. McLeod, Venice, CA: Lapis Press.

— (1990) *Heidegger and "the Jews"*, trans. Andreas Michel and Mark S Roberts, Minneapolis, MN: University of Minnesota Press.

— (1991) *The Inhuman: Reflections on Time*, trans. Geoffrey Bennington and Rachel Bowlby, Oxford: Blackwell.

— (1993) *Libidinal Economy*, trans. Iain Hamilton Grant, London: Athlone Press.

— (1993) *Political Writings*, Minneapolis, MN: University of Minnesota.

— (1993) *The Postmodern Explained to Children: Correspondence 1982–1985*, trans. Don Barry et al., Minneapolis, MN: University of Minnesota Press.

— (1993) *Toward the Postmodern*, Robert Harvey and Mark S. Roberts (eds), Atlantic Highlands, NJ and London: Humanities Press International.

— (1994) *Lessons on the Analytic of the Sublime*, trans. Elizabeth Rottenberg, Stanford, CA: Stanford University Press.

— (1997) *Postmodern Fables*, trans. George Van Den Abbeele, Minneapolis and London: University of Minnesota Press.

— (1997) 'The unconscious as mise-en-scène', in *Mimesis, masochism, & Mime: The Politics of Theatricality in Contemporary French Thought*, Timothy Murphy (ed.), Ann Arbor, MI: University of Michigan Press.

— (1998) *The Assassination of Experience by Painting – Monory*, trans. Rachel Bowlby, London: Black Dog.

— (1999) *Signed, Malraux*, trans. Robert Harvey, Minneapolis and London: University of Minnesota Press.

— (2006) *The Lyotard Reader and Guide*, eds James Williams and Keith Crome, Edinburgh: Edinburgh University Press.

— (2009) *Enthusiasm: The Kantian Critique of History*, trans. Georges Van Den Abbeele, Stanford, CA: Stanford University Press.

— (2009) 'Music and Postmodernity,' trans. David Bennett, in David Bennett (ed.), *Postmodernism, Music and Cultural Theory*, special issue of *New Formations*, 66 (Spring), pp.37–45.

— (2011) *Discourse, Figure*, Minneapolis: University of Minnesota Press.

— and Jean-Loup Thébald, (1985) *Just Gaming*, trans. Wlad Godzich, Manchester: Manchester University Press.

Mallarmé, Stéphane (2008) *Collected Poems and Other Verse*, Oxford World's Classics, Oxford.

Malpas, Simon (2003) *Jean-François Lyotard*, London: Routledge.

Merleau-Ponty, Maurice (1962) *Phenomenology of Perception*, trans. Colin Smith, London: Routledge & Kegan Paul.

Nietzsche, Friedrich (1968) *The Will to Power*, trans. Walter Kaufmann and R. J. Hollingdale, New York: Vintage Books.

— (1998) *Twilight of the Idols, or, How to Philosophize with a Hammer*, trans. Duncan Large, Oxford and New York: Oxford University Press.

Readings, Bill (1991) *Introducing Lyotard: Art and Politics*, London and New York: Routledge.

Richardson, John (2012) *Heidegger*, London: Routledge.

Saussure, Ferdinand (1966) *Course in General Linguistics*, trans. Wade Baskin, New York: McGraw-Hill.

Shaw, Philip (2006) *The Sublime*, London: Routledge.

Shlain, Leonard (1991) *Art and Physics: Parallel Visions in Space, Time and Light*, NY: William Morrow.

Silverman, Hugh J. (2002) *Lyotard: Philosophy, Politics and the Sublime*, New York: Routledge.

Sim, Stuart (1995) *Jean-François Lyotard*, New York: Prentice Hall and Harvester Wheatsheaf.

— (ed.) (2011) *The Lyotard Dictionary*, Edinburgh: Edinburgh University Press.

Slade, Andrew (2007) *Lyotard, Beckett, Duras, and the Postmodern Sublime*, New York: Peter Lang.

Stockhausen, Karlheinz (2002) "Huuuh!" Das Pressegespräch am 16. September 2001 im Senatszimmer des Hotel Atlantic in Hamburg" in *MusikTexte*, 91, pp.69–77.

Watts, Michael (2011) *The Philosophy of Martin Heidegger*, Montreal and Kingston: McGill-Queen's University Press.

Williams, James (1998) *Lyotard: Towards a Postmodern Philosophy*, Cambridge: Polity.

— (2000) *Lyotard and the Political*, London: Routledge.

Woodward, Ashley (2009) *Nihilism in Postmodernity*, Aurora, CO: The Davies Group.

— (2011) 'Nihilism and the sublime in Lyotard' in *Angelaki*, 16:2, pp.51–71.

Index